Urban Mobility Development in Northeast India

Urban Mobility Development in Northeast India theoretically and empirically explores the interrelationship between and among city, transportation, economic growth and environment to contribute towards engendering green urbanization for green growth.

In a time of aggravating environmental crisis, the book recognizes the duality of contrasting impact of city and transport to economic development and environmental degradation. To serve as a guide for policy research, the book accessibly presents a contextual study blending qualitative as well as quantitative methodology in the context of a highland as well as a frontier capital city of the Northeastern Indian state of Nagaland, Kohima, towards creating a sustainable city with an inclusive and green mobility. The book underscores that management of urbanization and urban mobility challenges should go beyond supply side management and demand side management by democratizing policy making as well as considering efficiency, equity, welfare and practicality concerns and suchlike rationales.

By traversing from abstraction to everyday life, from global context to frontier context and from macro level to micro level, the book makes significant theoretical as well as empirical contribution. The book will be of use to students, researchers, policy practitioners as well as general readers interested in Urban Studies, Transport Economics, Growth Economics, Development Studies, Environmental Studies and Asian Studies, especially in relation to highland and frontier regions in developing economies in general and Northeastern Region of India in particular.

Tumbenthung Y. Humtsoe currently works with the Government of Nagaland, India, as an Economics and Statistics Officer. He formerly taught at the National Institute of Technology (NIT), Nagaland, India.

Routledge Contemporary South Asia Series

For the full list of titles in the series please visit: www.routledge.com/
Routledge-Contemporary-South-Asia-Series/book-series/RCSA

Urban Mobility Development in Northeast India

Sustainable City with Green and Inclusive Transportation

Tumbenthung Y. Humtsoe

Routledge
Taylor & Francis Group

LONDON AND NEW YORK

First published 2024
by Routledge
4 Park Square, Milton Park, Abingdon, Oxon OX14 4RN

and by Routledge
605 Third Avenue, New York, NY 10158

Routledge is an imprint of the Taylor & Francis Group, an informa business

© 2024 Tumbenthung Y. Humtsoe

British Library Cataloguing-in-Publication Data
A catalogue record for this book is available from the British Library

ISBN: 978-1-032-71175-1 (hbk)
ISBN: 978-1-032-71177-5 (pbk)
ISBN: 978-1-032-71179-9 (ebk)

DOI: 10.4324/9781032711799

Typeset in Times New Roman
by Apex CoVantage, LLC

For
Kuvili
&
Amotsu osi Atsu
&
Apo osi Ayo and Ingu eno Ini

Contents

Figures

Tables

Abbreviations

AC	Average Cost
ASEAN	Association of Southeast Asian Nations
BPL	Below Poverty Line
BSF	Border Security Force
CBD	Central Business District
CO_2	Carbon Dioxide
DSM	Demand Side Management
ECS	Equivalent Car Space
GDP	Gross Domestic Product
GDI	Gender Development Index
GoI	Government of India
HDI	Human Development Index
HIG	High Income Group
HPI	Human Poverty Index
ICT	Information and Communications Technology
IT	Information Technology
KMC	Kohima Municipal Council
LIG	Low Income Group
MB	Marginal Benefit
MC	Marginal Cost
MIG	Middle Income Group
MPG	Marginally Poor Group
MSMEs	Micro, Small and Medium Enterprises
NEG	New Economic Geography
NER	Northeastern Region
NGOs	Non-governmental Organizations
NH	National Highway
NO_2	Nitrogen Dioxide
NPCB	Nagaland Pollution Control Board
PM	Particulate Matter
PTC	Private Trip Cost
PTS	Public Transportation System

RSPM	Respirable Suspended Particulate Matter
SO_2	Sulphur Dioxide
SPM	Suspended Particulate Matter
SSM	Supply Side Management
STC	Social Trip Cost
SWOT	Strengths, Weaknesses, Opportunities and Threats
UN	United Nations
UNDP	United Nations Development Program
US	United States

Preface

The going urbanization is a consequential phenomenon, on the nature of which depends the making of the development process of our present as well as our future sustainable. Discourses on the same as well as urbanism are therefore expectedly substantial. However, such discussions – academic as well as non-academic – are more often than not restricted to the epistemologically, geographically as well as ethnographically 'mainstream areas.' As a native researcher from an ethnographically as well as geographically 'periphery area,' such a limitation comes to pass as conspicuous in my readings of the scholarship within and outside the domain. The necessity (if not, desirability) to enrich the ongoing global discourse with contextual knowledge production from the frontier is immediately imperative. It is against the said backdrop that the present book is conceived by departing from the emphasis on large cities in the extant literature, and by deliberately engaging the theories of urbanization and urban mobility in the context of an under-researched region of Northeast India in general, and a still more under-researched highland as well as frontier capital city of the Northeastern Indian state of Nagaland, Kohima, in particular.

Any meaningful pursuit in life is ever done alone. Writing the book certainly was. To God be all the glory and honour, who – above and beyond all in all – blessed the following people along the way to whom I am penning to say, 'I am sincerely grateful.' Dr. Prajna Paramita Mishra, my amiable teacher, without whose invaluable guidance and support, the book would not have been possible. Dr. P. K. Mohanty, my inspirational teacher, who not only provided instrumental technical inputs but also drives me with his works and work ethics. Dr. Limakumba S. Walling, a teacher and a friend, for always being available when needed. Kuvili, for ever being my incisive reader and insightful reviewer. Ajung, Ethel, Jenithung, Menlom, Nuvitalu, Shomoi, Tsutsamo, Vungathung, William and Zareni, for the significant assistance during my fieldwork. Dorothea Schafter, senior editor at Taylor & Francis, whose valuable prompt guidance was instrumental in bringing the manuscript to publication. The anonymous readers whose careful reviews contributed much in sharpening up certain aspects of the book.

I have been loved by many. To all of you, I am ever grateful.

Tumbenthung
29 July 2023

Part I
Introduction

1   Green Urbanization
for Green Growth

Introduction

In the remarkable economic progress of humankind, transport and cities had been and continue to be significant drivers and facilitators. The many positive externalities (or simply, benefits and advantages) caused by an enhancement in transportation system had been of regional, national and international extent. By overcoming a spatial constraint, an advancement in the means of transportation – from a simple cart to the invention of a steam engine and later a jet engine – has continually brought a new possibility of division of labour (or simply, a separation of a process of work into a number of tasks), a diversification as well as a specialization of economic activities, economies of scale as well as economies of scope (while economies of scale refer to the fall in the cost of production owing to an increase in the scale of production, economies of scope refer to the fall in the cost of production owing to an increase in the variety of goods and services produced), and thereby causing economic growth as well as development. It is transport which provides the means for what economists have long perceived as an engine of growth, *intra-national and international trade*. By means of sea haulage, port cities of the past were prosperous centres of cultural and commercial exchange, providing inter alia rich revenue to royal exchequers. Urban agglomerations (as cities are often referred to in academic discourse) of today are the prime generators of the wealth of nations owing to the myriad agglomeration economies – the increasing returns (or simply, myriad benefits) that accrue to consumers, firms and industries, resulting from spatial agglomeration of producers and consumers.

Besides the aforesaid myriad positive externalities that transport and cities occasion, the same also create negative externalities (or simply, disadvantages and cost) including overcrowding, traffic congestion, pollution and so on. In a time of aggravating environmental crisis, the adverse ecological impacts of transport and cities have to be considered. The provision for mobility and urban space has been often at the cost of environment. Recognizing the contrasting impacts of transport and cities, the present book is, in essence, an optimization exercise towards maximizing the contribution from transport

DOI: 10.4324/9781032711799-2

and cities to economic as well as social development, while minimizing the contribution from the same to environmental degradation. In the said optimization exercise, urban mobility stands out because it simultaneously addresses the critical duality of aspects of any urban agglomeration's development: agglomeration economies (or cost saving owing to agglomeration of consumers and producers) enhancement and agglomeration diseconomies (or cost) mitigation. An efficient urban mobility system plying on an adequately connected network of roads contributes to the *liveability*, *efficiency*, *competitiveness* and *sustainability* of an urban agglomeration. In essence, urban mobility development and management strategy can and should address the concerns of a socially inclusive as well as an environmentally sustainable economic growth.

Studies that combine Growth Economics, Urban Economics, Transport Economics and Environmental Economics to derive policy lessons for urban mobility development and management strategy is scant, more so in the context of the under-researched Northeastern Region (hereafter NER) of India. Alluding to the region's ethnography, geography as well as the existing socio-economic and political state of affairs, NER is generally and variedly referred to as an *ethnogeographic periphery* (Agrawal and Kumar, 2020) or a *landlocked hilly state* (Agrawal and Kumar, 2020) or a *troubled periphery* – given the ethnic conflict as well as the insurgency-related problems in the region (Sarmah, 2020) or a *geo-politically sequestered* region (Government of India, hereafter GoI, 1997) as well as an *infrastructural deficit* region (GoI, 1997). 'Most academic studies on India that rely on statistics limit themselves to "major" states for want of data and exclude the North-eastern region' (Agrawal and Kumar, 2020).

The extant literature on urbanism in the region is expectedly limited in extent as well as scope. 'The rapid urbanization of India's Northeast frontier is one of the most crucial transformations the area has witnessed, yet it remains relatively understudied . . . Urban environments are rarely part of imaginations of the frontier' (McDuie-Ra, 2017). The scant studies on urbanization in NER are limited to providing an account of the shared as well as distinct historical and contemporary drivers of urbanization, socio-economic and administrative characteristics of urban agglomerations (Singh and Singha, 2020; Xaxa, 2019; McDuie-Ra, 2017, Dikshit and Dikshit, 2013; Khawas, 2005), urban water and waste management in larger cities in the region such as Guwahati (Singh and Singha, 2020), governance of urban space by multiple stakeholders in relation to another larger city of Shillong (Xaxa, 2019), and suchlike. What emerges from the extant literature is therefore a conspicuous absence of a research on urban mobility in the NER, notwithstanding the critical salience of urban transportation in the form and shape a city takes, and accordingly the quality of life in such a city (as explicated in the book).

It further appears that the planning and development strategies of the cities in the region have neither considered nor incorporated fundamental elements from the theories and applications of the aforementioned domains of

Economics. Specifically, an integrated agglomeration-transport-environment strategy is found evidently absent. Against such a backdrop of research gap, and the corollary lack of informed policy making and intervention, the book is conceived in the context of a highland as well as a frontier capital city of the Northeastern Indian state of Nagaland (as detailed later in the current chapter as well as in the ensuing chapters). After establishing theoretically as well as empirically that urbanization can be construed as a green resource for sustainable development, a focus on making the same in the context of Kohima is made with an emphasis on urban mobility.

'For long, official and academic discourse on the issues of development in Nagaland and the Northeastern region centred, perhaps justifiably, on the "security-development nexus" (Mishra and Upadhyay, 2017) and centre-periphery relations' (Walling and Humtsoe, 2021). The book therefore takes a break from such problematizations and introduces a new dimension to the ongoing discourse on development with respect to an infrastructural deficit frontier economy characterized by contextual specificities (with unique challenges as well as opportunities, and therefore unique policy priorities). A study of the nature discussed in the book exists neither in the context of the subject city of Kohima nor in the case of the state of Nagaland. Moreover, the book can serve as a guide for policy research in cities that share comparable geography as well as socio-political and economic reality.

Theory guides praxis and praxis enriches theory. It is critical to appreciate the interrelated nature of the connection between and among urbanization, urban mobility, growth and environment (as explored in the book), and combine the same with contextual empirical evidence in policy formulation and intervention to engender an *agglomeration economies augmenting, congestion diseconomies* (drawbacks and cost) *mitigating*, and *resource generating city*. By traversing from an abstraction to an everyday life, from a global context to a frontier context and from a macro level to a micro level, the book is conceived to make an important theoretical as well as empirical contribution towards creating a green urbanization for a green growth.

All the aforementioned sub-disciplines of Economics, save Growth Economics, are basically applications of Microeconomics principles.

Growth Economics Perspective

How does an economy grow? The said question encompasses the subject matter of Growth Economics. Different theories of growth espoused by different scholars emphasize different causes of growth. For the expansion of the wealth of nations, while most economists (including those subscribing to Neoclassical Economics) emphasize on the supply side factors (such as an enhancement in labour productivity causing an economic growth), others (including those subscribing to Keynesian Economics) emphasize on the demand side factors (such as an augmented demand – from either a creation of a new market or an expansion of an existing market – stimulating economic growth). By corollary, either supply side constraints to economic growth or demand side limits to growth (or both) can arise in different circumstances.

In an economic growth modelling, usually expressed in terms of a function, the drivers of growth (supply side drivers or demand side factors) are conceived as either endogenous or exogenous. While endogenous growth models assume that sole factors within an economic system result in an economic growth (by internal and interdependent factors), exogenous growth models assume that economic growth arises owing to influences outside an economy (by external and independent factors). Institutions therefore assume a critical role in the exogenous models of growth.

While the question relating to *how cities and transport engender and contribute to economic growth* is answered by Urban Economics and Transport Economics respectively, Environmental Economics answers the question pertaining to *how to make economic growth environmentally sustainable*.

Urban Economics Perspective

How do utility-maximizing households and profit-maximizing firms make locational choices? Urban Economics explores the said question by marrying the disciplines of Economics and Geography. An urban agglomeration comes about as well as expands owing to agglomeration economies. Agglomeration economies are the productivity benefits and cost savings that spring from the co-location of firms, workers and different institutions within a particular agglomeration centre. Spatial contiguity, proximity and density enable and foster contacts, collaborations and learning. In such ways, cities facilitate *economies of learning*, *matching* (say, between employers and employees), *sharing* as well as *networking*. Agglomeration causes a reduction in cost of transporting not only people as well as goods and services, but also information (or knowledge). Urban Economics, in essence, combines the conceptions of agglomeration externalities from New Economic Geography and knowledge externalities from Endogenous Growth Models to explain why economic activities cluster spatially, and consequently engender a city.

On the contrary, agglomeration diseconomies (including overcrowding, house rent increasing beyond the reach of the masses, polluted ambient air, to mention notable few) act as centripetal forces. Beyond a certain optimal threshold, such negative externalities of spatial clustering give rise to an increased cost of production and living as well as a reduced quality of life. Such an optimum threshold can be, however, extended by means of an effective implementation of an efficiently designed urban planning. It is therefore imperative to maximize agglomeration economies and minimize agglomeration diseconomies. The quality of urban life is contingent on the success of such an optimization.

Transport Economics Perspective

Beginning from the source of raw materials through the processes of production and distribution and up to the final consumption, a transport flow occurs throughout the entire stretch of a supply chain. Transport can be therefore viewed as an input (or as a cost) in production and distribution, and thereby requiring an optimization (Batta, 2008). Against such a background, Transport Economics is concerned with the myriad positive externalities (as well as negative externalities – as discussed in the following) connected to a transportation system (such as transport network externalities and wider area benefits from transportation system). For producers or suppliers, benefits of economies of scale as well as economies of scope arise by means of an access to a new market or a larger market (including a previously inaccessible labour pool) brought about by an enhancement in transportation infrastructure and services. For the consumers, either a reduction or a rise in transport cost is passed on to them – in terms of lower or higher price – as purchasers of final goods and services. Furthermore, economies of density (expressly, increasing returns to traffic density) are engendered with an increase in the transportation services within a network of a given size. The suppliers as well as consumers benefit by means of an availability of greater connectivity choices – *convenience benefit* – with such an increase in the number of network connections as well as logistical and conveyance services.

On the contrary, an inefficiently complex transport network as well as an inefficient transportation management can cause an avoidable economic and environmental cost – in the forms of traffic congestion, traffic accidents, vehicular air pollution, fragmentation of forest and so on. An economically efficient, socially inclusive as well as environmentally sustainable transportation system can minimize such cost on the one hand, and maximize network externalities as well as other suchlike positive economies on the other hand.

Environmental Economics Perspective

The economic systems and environmental systems are closely intertwined. To fully comprehend as well as factor such systems, Economics must incorporate the mechanical underpinnings of the natural sciences, and the natural sciences must incorporate the behavioural underpinnings of Economics (Hanley et al., 2004). While the behavioural underpinnings suggest that an economic agent generally responds to incentives (in the sense that, while making a decision, costs and benefits are weighed) and typically acts in self-interest, the mechanical underpinnings suggest that environmental resources are limited and the uses of the same have opportunity cost (such as an irreversible loss of an ecosystem service or a keystone species). Against such a backdrop, market failures (for instance, a failure to account for the cost of pollution) as well as government failures (say, by distorting market responsiveness to an increasing scarcity) have resulted in too many environmental bads. Markets, which have 'proved to be the best way of allocating a vast range of resources' (Hanley et al., 2004), should be made to work for environment by means of an appropriate pricing as well as by converging the divergence between private cost and social cost (as explained in a later chapter in the context of commuting). Making the market work may entail a varying degree of either a governmental intervention in certain cases or a governmental withdrawal in certain cases.

Having presented the global contextual motivations of the book, the national as well as regional milieus under which the book is envisaged are discussed in the following. The ensuing sections are so ordered as to methodically introduce the subject city, Kohima, the capital city of the Northeastern Indian state of Nagaland.

Economic Growth, Urbanization and Urban Mobility in India

Indian economy has grown rapidly in recent memory and is, at the time of scripting the book, the fastest growing large economy in the world. Driven by the ongoing growth, urban spaces are sprouting and enlarging at a rapid pace in India. Between 1901 and 2011, the number of such spaces increased by three times. Suggesting an enlargement of the existing urban spaces, urban population expanded by 13 times during the same period. Such an already expanded urban population is further projected to more than double between 2011 and 2050 – from 377 million to 814 million (Mohanty and Mishra, 2017). The growing economy as well as the expanding urban population is increasingly causing a surge in mobility demand. Urban mobility scenario in India is, however, beset with many concerns and challenges.

Against the background of a quantitatively as well as qualitatively inadequate Public Transportation System (PTS) and a non-motorized mobility infrastructure, the mushrooming of personalized modes of mobility on a largely static road capacity sans an adequate parking space is accentuating the already severe traffic congestion as well as the already contaminated urban environment owing to vehicular pollution. For a further discussion on the major challenges (including on environmental aspects) for sustainable transport in the context of urban India, see Anbalagan (2012). All this reflects a failure in policy aspect: an absence of an integrated spatial-transport planning, an under-investment in transport infrastructure and services as well as a deficiency in institutional mechanism.

The existing inadequate state of urban mobility is a primary constraint in realizing the potential of an urban agglomeration as a green engine of growth for 'urban transport is the artery of urban economy which is also an integral part of overall economy' (Anbalagan, 2012). '[I]nadequate infrastructure investments in cities might have inhibited secondary and tertiary sectors growth, leading to too few jobs being generated in the non-agricultural economy' (Mohanty, 2014). Furthermore, cities in India are going from bad to worse apropos environment, with some of the most polluted cities in the world found in the country. Far from being sustainable growth centres, such cities are therefore economically performing sub-optimally and environmentally faring worryingly. Some of such concerns are more pronounced in the much more inadequately connected NER of India.

Economic Growth, Urbanization and Urban Mobility in Northeastern India

Northeastern India is grossly underdeveloped, with the economies of the eight states in the region comparing poorly with the rest of the Indian states in terms of broad macroeconomic indicators. The comparative disparity is more marked in the aspect of infrastructure, particularly in connectivity. The NER consequently remains largely agrarian and mostly inaccessible. Given the economic backwardness, the process of urbanization in NER has been sluggish as compared to national average (see Figure 1.1), and the region is the least urbanized in India.

The relatively sluggish urbanization that is occurring in the region is, however, marked by a variety of problems: 'from urban environment to security and from lack of infrastructure to social conflict' (Khamrang, 2012). A past observation made by Asian Development Bank (2004) that 'urban infrastructure and service are grossly inadequate in the capital cities of Northeast India'

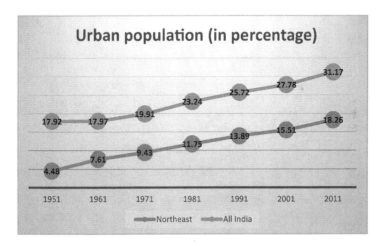

Figure 1.1 Urban population of Northeastern Region vis-à-vis All India (in percentage)
Source: Devi (2012)

remains largely valid even at the present. In the main, urban road capacity is quantitatively as well as qualitatively inadequate, with the existing road network as well as parking space falling short of the demand arising from the current traffic volume – which has rapidly increased in recent years. Another past observation made by Asian Development Bank (2004) that 'cities in Northeast attract large chunk of migrants from the surrounding areas but failed to provide basic amenities and services leading to urban involution, congestion and decay' remains largely valid even nowadays.

In the ongoing Act East Policy (a policy of Government of India – previously called Look East Policy – with an aim to promote economic cooperation, cultural connection and strategic relationship with East Asian countries through an enhanced connectivity with the states of NER of India), the cities of Northeast India are viewed as centres of investment to propel the regional economy. Towards the same direction, an 'investment in urban infrastructure [particularly in transport] and services will be the key to unleashing the potential of these cities to crystallize the growth of Northeast region' (Asian Development Bank, 2004). Accordingly, such an investment imperative also emerges from an overview of the state of urbanism in a highland state of NER, Nagaland.

Economic Growth and Urbanism in Nagaland

Comparable to the economies in the region, the current state of Nagaland's economy is characterized by unutilized and underutilized growth potential. Notwithstanding the rich natural endowments (such as forest resources, mineral resources, favourable agro-climatic as well as soil conditions and tourism prospect) as well as an educated human resource, the state has been unable to leverage the same for economic development. 'Nagaland still remains underdeveloped and inaccessible' (Government of Nagaland, hereafter GoN, 2004). While concluding that 'it is necessary to stimulate the secondary [sector],' the Vision 2030 document of GoN (2016) suggests that industrialization will not ensue until the necessary infrastructures and institutional environments are provided. Reviewing the macroeconomic indicators of Nagaland for a decade (from 1994 to 2014), Walling and Humtsoe (2021) concluded that the state's economic development is in 'doldrums.'

Urbanization is, however, a given phenomenon in the underdeveloped state as well. In 2001, 20% of the population lived in urban space (GoI, 2001), which increased to 29% in 2011 (GoI, 2011). 'The urbanization pattern is [however] somewhat skewed as the urban growth is concentrated in few key towns such as Dimapur and Kohima' (GoN, 2016). Accordingly, the difference in the state of urbanization between that of Kohima district and that of the state doubled – from 8% in 2001 to a little more than 16% in 2011 (GoI, 2011).

Given the skewed nature of urbanization against a backdrop of an economic backwardness and stagnation, it is only expected to observe deficiencies in critical urban services in such concentrated urban growth centres. Accordingly, a grossly inadequate PTS, a burgeoning number of private cars on a largely stagnant road capacity, a worsening traffic congestion as well as an aggravating vehicular pollution, an increasing water scarcity, a hazardous sewage disposal, and other suchlike concerns plague the cities and towns of the state. All this is observed at a magnified proportion in the subject city of Kohima.

Economic Growth and Urbanism in Kohima

Kohima is an important centre of agglomeration in the state as well as in the entire NER. It is a centre of administration, healthcare and education as well as an important large market in the region. Although it has been a driver of growth for the state as well as the region, its potential to propel the economic growth of the state as well as the region has not been realized to the maximum, and therefore presents an opportunity.

Given the acute infrastructural shortage, Kohima appears as though it has 'grown beyond [its] carrying capacities' (GoN, 2016). Urban challenges confronting the city consist of: 'acute water shortage problems along with problems of garbage,' land as well as house rent 'becoming beyond the reach of the common man,' and exacerbating air pollution (GoN, 2016). Among such concerns, however, the 'clogged' (GoN, 2016) flow of traffic in the street is holding the city in a standstill. Reflecting all this is the infamy of Kohima as the second most *unliveable* city in India (expressly, for poor scores in the components of the Ease of Living Index: *quality of life, economic ability* and *sustainability*) (GoI, 2018, 2019). The prevailing state undoubtedly presents not only a policy challenge but also an opportunity to leverage the ongoing agglomeration in the city as a *green resource* for socio-economic development. In that direction, the need for an apropos urban mobility policy intervention cannot be overemphasized to make the city going and running.

More aspects concerning Kohima – a history of urbanization as well as connectivity, a socio-economic as well as spatial profile, and so on – are detailed in a later chapter.

Conceptual Frame and Methodology

The book presents a multidisciplinary as well as a contextual policy research blending quantitative as well as qualitative methodology with a sound theoretical foundation (as briefed earlier) to draw policy lessons for a sustainable city with an inclusive and green mobility. For studying urbanism as well as urban mobility concerns in the context of a frontier economy, while the theoretical work is suitably framed, the empirical work is also appropriately constructed – departing from conventional designs, as detailed later in the relevant chapter on praxis. The available secondary data (including government documents as and where available) employed in the study is supplemented by qualitative data from personal observations. Notably, given the absence of a study of the nature carried out in the book (specifically, in the context of Kohima), the pioneering study is primarily carried out by employing primary data obtained by means of a questionnaire-based survey. Responses from stakeholders are obtained by means of structured as well as unstructured and open-ended interviews – in order to capture unconventional yet pertinent responses from lived realities of the stakeholders. A detailed discussion on the sampling strategy as well as the employment of the so-collected data is made in the ensuing relevant chapter in the book.

Organization of the Book

A broad introduction to the book is presented in the current introductory *Chapter 1* of *Part I* of the book. *Part II* (comprising *Chapters 2* and *3*) discusses the theories of urbanization, urban mobility, growth and environment. A new multidisciplinary context-specific conceptual framework is proposed in *Part II* to study the concerns and challenges associated with urbanization (in the main in developing economies), informed by theoretical perspectives from Growth Economics, Environmental Economics, Urban Economics and Transport Economics. *Part III* (consisting of *Chapters 4, 5* and *6*) discusses the praxis of development and management of urban agglomeration. A departure from the emphasis on large cities in the extant literature is made in *Part III*, and an attention is drawn to the rapidly emerging concerns of urbanization in emerging cities of developing economies. As such, the empirical work is carried out in the context of an under-researched Northeastern Indian state of Nagaland, and thereby making the book a pioneering work of Economics (specifically on urbanization) in relation to the region as well as the state. It draws attention to the unique contextual processes driving the emerging urbanization challenges in a highland city at the frontier, and correspondingly emphasizes the contextually unique mitigation measures warranted therefrom. Reiterating the findings of the study, *Chapter 7* of *Part IV* concludes the book.

The chapter outlines are briefed as follows.

A growing economy in a salubrious environment is imperative. It entails that not all growth paths are apposite. To get to an apposite growth path, as close as possible, a prior exploration of the dynamics between and among economic growth, environment, transport and city is imperative. That is done in *Chapter 2*. A bidirectional causality nature of relationship exists between the aforesaid variables. Such a nature of interrelationship should be appreciated in policy formulation and intervention.

Chapter 2 explores urbanization as a *green resource* for a sustainable development. It is critical to comprehend the economic rationales for spatial organization of economic activities in an urban agglomeration to appreciate as well as leverage urbanization as a resource for sustainable economic growth. The multifarious positive externalities that a city occasion can be appreciated through a frame of a metaphorical inverted pyramid, starting with the spatial organization of production under a singular roof, and then in an industrial district and finally in a city. Validating such theoretical expectations is today's economic reality (as borne out by empirical evidence) wherein cities are the prime generators of the wealth of nations.

As an introductory chapter of the praxis part of the book, *Chapter 4* provides a historical context as well as a spatial and socio-economic profile of Kohima in order to set a stage for an empirical enquiry of urbanism concerning the said city. The application of SWOT (strengths, weaknesses, opportunities and threats) assessment of a city for an urban policy making is then demonstrated – expressly, as an initial study to identify the challenges and prospects of a sustainable development of a city. Although the employment of SWOT in urban planning is not common, it can be gainfully employed for the same as shown in the chapter. Given the absence of an informed policy intervention in Kohima, SWOT analysis of the city is made to come up with a comprehensively integrated and an effective city development strategy.

An application of theory to praxis (expressly, traffic congestion alleviation) is illustrated in *Chapter 5*. Traffic congestion has a bearing on growth as well as environment; and therefore, the mitigation of the same is economically and environmentally imperative. Such an exercise is accordingly taken up in the context of Kohima. In the said exercise, an overall picture of the state of urban mobility in the city becomes clear. A theoretical model based on an extended speed function (as distinct from the standard speed function, and as explained later in the chapter) and a traffic demand curve is developed to demonstrate that in a scenario such as Kohima characterized by an acute supply side bottleneck, supply side interventions should precede pricing and regulation for efficiency, welfare, practicality challenges and other suchlike rationales. A unique situation calls for a unique policy intervention. As such, a policy intervention should be preceded by an analysis of the nature made for the case of Kohima.

For effective congestion mitigation, feasible inputs from the commuters should be incorporated in supply side management as well as demand side management to bring about a consumer-relevant and an effective improvement in urban mobility. Accordingly, *Chapter 6* demonstrates an empirical attempt towards making evidence-based and effective demand side transport management strategy. Given the severe traffic congestion in Kohima, a *bivariate logit travel mode choice model*[1] based on an urban transport sample survey is conceived. The dependent variable (alternative transport mode choice) therefore takes either a congestion accentuating mode or a congestion easing mode.

Leveraging the rapidly occurring urbanization as a green resource through an agglomeration economies augmenting, congestion diseconomies mitigating and resource generating city will generate a substantial opportunity for poverty reduction, rural development and, on the whole, an economic development. Giving a general contour of the various findings of the study, *Chapter 7* concludes the book with directions for future research.

Note

1 A bivariate logit model estimates the probability of either of the duality of events taking place (in the present context, either a congestion accentuating mode or a congestion easing mode).

References

Agrawal, Ankush and Kumar, Vikas, *Numbers in India's periphery: the political economy of government statistics*. Cambridge University Press, Cambridge, 2020.

Anbalagan, P, *Urban development and sustainable transport*. Bookwell Publications, New Delhi, 2012.

Asian Development Bank, *India: North-eastern region urban development*. Asian Development Bank, 2004. www.adb.org/projects/35290-012/main

Batta, Ravinder N, *Economics of the road transport*. Kalpaz Publications, Delhi, 2008.

Devi, Bimolata K, *A study on urbanization in North-eastern states of India*. International Journal of Current Research, 4(10), 272–276, 2012.

Dikshit, K R and Dikshit, J K, *Urbanisation and urban landscape in Northeast India*. In Northeast India: land, people and economy. Advances in Asian Human-Environmental Research, Springer, Dordrecht, 2013. https://doi.org/10.1007/978-94-007-7055-3_15

Government of India, *Census of India*. Government of India, 2001. http://censusindia.gov.in/

Government of India, *Census of India*. Government of India, 2011. http://censusindia.gov.in/

Government of India, *Ease of living index*. Government of India, 2018. https://amplifi.mohua.gov.in/eol-landing

Government of India, *Ease of living index*. Government of India, 2019. https://amplifi.mohua.gov.in/eol-landing

Government of India, *Transforming the Northeast, tackling backlogs in basic minimum services and infrastructural needs: high level commission report to the Prime Minister*. Government of India, 1997. https://planningcommission.nic.in/reports/genrep/ne_exe.pdf

Government of Nagaland, *Nagaland state human development report*. Government of Nagaland, 2004. www.in.undp.org/

Government of Nagaland, *Nagaland vision 2030*. Government of Nagaland, 2016. www.nagaland.gov.in/

Hanley, Nick, Shorgen, Jason F and White, Ben, *Introduction to environmental economics*. Oxford University Press Inc., New York, 2004.

Khamrang, Leishipem, *Perceived quality of life in the cities of Northeast India: a welfare geographical perspective*. International Journal of Social Science Tomorrow, 1(3), 1–9, 2012.

Khawas, Vimal, *Urbanisation in the Northeast: patterns, trends, and policy prongs*. Social Change, 35, 47–69, 2005. www.researchgate.net/publication/258185501_ Urbanisation_in_the_North East_Patterns_trends_and_policy_prongs

McDuie-Ra, Duncan, *Learning to love the city in Northeast India*. The Newsletter. International Institute for Asian Studies, 2017. www.iias.asia/thenewsletter/article/ learning-love-city-northeast-india

Mishra, K. Deepak and Upadhyay, Vandana, *Rethinking economic development in Northeast India: The emerging dynamics*. Routledge, India, 2017.

Mohanty, Prasanna K, *Cities and public policy: an urban agenda for India*. Sage India, New Delhi, 2014.

Mohanty, Prasanna K and Mishra, Alok, *Urbanisation and land: challenges for smart cities in India*. HSMI and HUDCO Chair- University of Hyderabad Collaboration Research, 2017.

Sarmah, Bhupen, *Global governance and India's Northeast: logistics, infrastructure and society* (edited by Ranabir Samaddar and Anita Sengupta, Routledge, 2019). Social Change and Development, XVII, 0975–4016, 2020.

Singh, Amarjeet M and Singha, Komol, *Understanding urbanisation in Northeast India: issues and challenges*. Routledge, New Delhi, 2020.

Walling, Limakumba S and Humtsoe, Tumbenthung Y, *Political economy of development in the Indian state of Nagaland: issues and challenges*. Indian Journal of Human Development, Sage, 15(3), 395–409, 2021.

Xaxa, Aashish, *Tribes and urbanisation in Northeast India: issues and challenges*. Economic and Political Weekly, 54(38), 2019. www.epw.in/journal/2019/38/special-articles/tribes-and-urbanisation-north-east-india.html

Part II
Theory

2 Apposite Economic Growth Path

Introduction

Throughout history, humankind has been altering environment to its comfort, or in Economics lexicon, in the pretext of economic growth and development. Especially since the *industrial revolution*, the extraction of natural resources as well as modification of nature have been proceeding at an increasing proportion. Humankind has shaped the earth to such an extent that a new human-moulded geologic epoch, the *anthropocene*, has dawned. Although much has been achieved in terms of material wellbeing, it is not without a cost to the environment. An extension of transportation network as well as an expansion of urban space account to a large extent in bringing about an adverse environmental change.

We are living in a time of environmental crisis. The increasing understanding of the emerging reality of the same generated a new discourse that attempts to shift away from the dominant anthropocentric view to a broader ecological perspective of assessing human material progress. 'By the 1960s, the adverse environmental impact of unbridled economic growth was becoming clear. Books like Rachel Carson's Silent Spring set the tone for an environmental movement' (Rajagopalan, 2011). Such a change in perspective was followed by an international collective action to address the evolving concern. The United Nations' Conference on Human Environment conducted in Stockholm in 1972 was the notable beginning of such a global initiative. The next development of consequential salience was the constitution of the World Commission on Environment and Development in 1987, a report of which, *Our Common Future*, 'emphasized the need for an integration of economic and ecological systems' (Rajagopalan, 2011). The report also 'defined and supported the concept of sustainable development' (Rajagopalan, 2011). The Paris Climate Accord in 2015 – to restrict global rise in temperature to well below 2 degrees Celsius – is the most recent significant development.

Specifically on urbanization, under the United Nations' (2016) New Urban Agenda, the member states committed to preserve and promote the 'ecological and social function of land in cities,' and to facilitate the sustainable management of natural resources in such settlements in a manner that 'protects

DOI: 10.4324/9781032711799-4

and improves the urban ecosystem and environmental services and reduces greenhouse gas emissions and air pollution.' Although *sustainability* as a policy objective is now increasingly emphasized in policy discourse, the same has not been translated into policy intervention at a warranted proportion.

A growing economy in a salubrious environment is imperative. It entails that not all growth paths are apposite. To get to an apposite growth path, as close as possible, the need for a prior exploration of the relationship between economic growth and environment cannot be overstated. Analogously, surveying the dynamics between and among transport, city, economic growth and environment is essential. Accordingly, the present chapter attempts to inquire the interrelationship among the same.

Economic Growth and Environment

On the one hand, a review of the extant literature suggests an argument in the nature of *environment versus economic growth* (or development). A view espoused by *Degrowth* and other similar approaches, it essentially postulates a trade-off between environment and growth. Given such a trade-off, the imperative of an expanding economy in a salubrious environment presents a dilemma for policy makers. For simultaneously pursuing an economic growth as well as an environmental protection is problematic – given the possibility that the pursuit of the former objective may hinder the realization of the latter objective, and vice versa.

On the other hand, some literature suggests an argument in the nature of *environment and growth* (or development), arguing that growth and environmental protection (say, through regulations) are simultaneously possible. And that considering the problem as a trade-off is a fallacy (see Porter, 1990; Templet, 1995; Feiock and Stream, 2001). 'Recent studies report positive cross-sectional correlations between . . . environmental protection and personal income (Feiock and Stream, 2001). In the context of the state of Nagaland as well, Humtsoe (2020) observes '[that] there are also cases where [deficiency] of development and not development per se is detrimental to environment can be appreciated from an observation in [a town in the state].' Although such a categorization of the extant literature runs the risk of oversimplification, the current section is entitled *Economic Growth and Environment* subscribing to the latter nature of argument.

Economic growth – an increase in the output of goods and services in an economy – comes about because of either an increase in input or a technological progress (productivity enhancements[1]), or both occurring simultaneously. Concurrently, the said duality of factors can create either a limit (ceiling) or slowdown (deceleration) in economic growth. An illustration of the same can be made by employing Cobb-Douglas production function (a production function is an equation representing a technological relationship between output produced and inputs employed. Cobb-Douglas production function is a widely used particular form of such a production function), which can be expressed as follows:

$$Q_t = Ae^{rt} K_t^{a1} L_t^{a2} E_t^{a3} O_t^{a4},$$

where Q is the output; K, L, E and O are capital, labour, energy and other resources respectively (or collectively, input); A, a1, a2, a3, a4 and r are all constants; and t is the current year.

With an increase in such inputs, if the sum of the *a* exponents is equal to 1, a constant returns to scale exists (meaning, the increase in the cost of inputs is equal to the increase in the value of output); if it is greater than 1, an increasing returns to scale exists (meaning, the increase in the value of output is more than the increase in the value of inputs); and if it is less than 1, a diminishing returns to scale exists (meaning, the increase in the cost of inputs is more than the increase in the value of output).

To bring out the role of technical progress, the above equation can be rewritten in the form of a growth rate as follows:

$$Q'/Q = r + a_1 K'/K + a_2 L'/L + a_3 E'/E + a_4 O'/O^2$$

It can be inferred from the above equation that the rate of growth of output (Q'/Q) is equal to a weighted sum of the growth rate of individual inputs and that of r, which is taken to represent a technical progress. As long as r > 0, growth thereby occurs, even if the other independent variables in the equation remain constant.

In the historical process of economic growth – in the employment of inputs and technology being used – too many environmental bads have been produced alongside too few environmental goods. It is not always so, however, that an economic growth causes environmental bads. An absence of the former also causes the latter. That a 'deforestation is caused in part by the migration of landless peasants into the forests, seeking a plot of land to work' (Sinha and Nongpluh, 2014) is an example. Analogously, the most polluted cities in the world are not found in rich countries, but in poor countries (Tietenberg, 2003). Accordingly, 'dealing effectively with these environmental problems, and the human sufferings that lies behind them, will require raising living standards' (Tietenberg, 2003), which is possible only with economic growth and development. All this follows the view of *economic growth and environment* as opposed to *economic growth versus environment*.

Going forward, inputs substitutability and technological progress will determine whether the economic growth runs either the course of an environmentally sustainable *green path* or that of an environmentally unsustainable *brown path*. Of prime importance in the present context is the case of whether capital and conventional energy (or specifically, fossil fuel, which has contributed much and continues to accentuate global warming) would remain complementary, or whether capital (a reproducible asset) will substitute such irreproducible conventional energy, and *fuel* the growth process either with a reduced emission or without an emission – a case of a continually decreasing carbon footprint growth pathway. If an environmental imperative of either a continual reduction in the use of fossil fuel or a substitution of brown fuel by a green fuel is not affected – and the conventional energy continues to be complementary to capital, then the trade-off between economic growth and environment will remain (Tietenberg, 2003).

A technological progress causing an enhancement in the productivity of a conventional energy input (say, by means of a more fuel-efficient machinery) not only contributes to solving the impending absolute bound to economic growth from the finiteness of environmental resources but also contributes to mitigating environmental pollution. Against such a backdrop, the ongoing technological innovation that is continually creating a *greener* technology, an enhancement in the productivity of conventional energy input (expressly, carbon energy) and in harnessing non-conventional sources of energy input is welcomed. In perspective, the continual possibility for a green growth exists in such innovative developments. For a further detailed discussion on the challenges, institutional frameworks and policies (including success stories as well as best practices) for such a low-carbon pathway for transportation in emerging countries (expressly, Brazil, China, India, Mexico and Turkey), see Lah (2018).

Transportation and Economic Growth

The primary function of transport is to provide connectivity between spatially separated locations as well as for the movement of freights (inputs and outputs) and passengers for business sector and household sector. Accordingly, it plays a foremost part in an interaction between market size on the demand side and specialization on the supply side that contributes to economic growth. Analogously, such a synergic relationship between transport and growth is discussed further in the following.

Reduction in Generalized Costs

Any enhancement in transportation system initially affects the generalized cost of travel for existing transport users, which in turn translates into various downstream effects on the economy, which Eddington (2006) terms as 'micro-economic drivers of productivity or micro drivers mechanisms' – enumerated in the following:

'(a) Increasing business efficiency through 'time savings' and improved reliability for business travellers, freight and logistics operations; (b) Increasing business investment and innovation by supporting economies of scale or new ways of working; (c) Supporting clusters and agglomerations of economic activity; (d) Improving the efficient functioning of labour markets, increasing labour market flexibility and the accessibility of jobs; (e) Increasing competition by opening up access to new markets; (f) Increasing domestic and international trade by reducing the costs of trading; (g) Attracting globally mobile activity . . . by providing an attractive business environment and good quality of life' (Eddington, 2006).

Transportation and Productive Capacity

An efficient transportation system expands an economy's productive capacity by enhancing the mobilization and productivity of available resources – in response to globalization, new technological opportunities, prospects of part-time as well as full-time participation in labour markets (especially, female participation) located in different spaces, and so on (Eddington, 2006). Without an adequate provision of transportation system, *capabilities* (expressly, universal education and universal healthcare) would be practically impossible to attain for want of an accessibility to interior areas, or to bring other such socio-welfare services to people residing in either a previously insufficiently accessible or a completely inaccessible area.

Transportation and Agglomeration Economies

The continual overcoming of the constraint of distance that an augmentation in transport system engenders causes scale economies. The consequent fall in the cost of transportation as well as the rise in the ease of movement contribute to market expansion including development of new market, and transform an otherwise unattractive location into an attractive location in terms of private investment – thereby bringing employment opportunities. Such an improvement can expand labour market catchment, improve job matching and facilitate business-to-business interactions. All this further occasions specialization, knowledge spillovers and other such agglomeration economies.

An accessible land is generally put to an optimum use, and therefore tends to be more developed. Such a land receives an *accessibility premium* (say, in the form of a higher rent), which an inaccessible land does not. A region with a relatively better accessibility, ceteris paribus, attracts resources from other regions causing further agglomeration – a case of a sort of Myrdal's (1944) cumulative causation of growth. A policy implication may be of note from the same, as it occasions a possibility of skewed regional development, which assumes an even greater salience in the context of economic liberalization, with the private sector (the investment in which and from which positively correlates to accessibility) being envisioned as the prime mover of the economy.

Spatial Effects of Transportation

Transportation forms an important factor in determining spatial location of economic activities as well as population centres. A transport system is an input to a household's consumption decision as well as to a firm's investment decision. Any changes in the input (variations in the availability and quality of mobility system) therefore crucially influence the spatial decisions of households and firms, which are reflected in the migration of existing firms and households, establishment of new firms, fixed capital investment in different locations, and so on.

For firms, locating in urban concentrations may mean neglecting interior markets. In such a consideration for a locational decision, transport cost becomes 'important in determining the balance between agglomeration and dispersion forces, as both forces diminish as transport and trade costs decline' (Government of New Zealand, 2014). A corollary question then arises: under what conditions does transportation investment benefit a target region? Standing Advisory Committee on Trunk Road Appraisal of the Government of United Kingdom (hereafter SACTRA, 1999) suggested the following. To begin with, where scale economies dominate, a lower transport cost through an improved accessibility may encourage an increased concentration of firms in a core region, until a threshold where diseconomies set in. Next, the larger the size of local market, the larger an agglomeration force. Then, the better the condition of local land as well as that of local labour, the larger an agglomeration force. Next, the better the nature of backward linkages as well as forward linkages (while backward linkages refer to the interrelationship of a firm or an industry with other firms or industries from which it buys its inputs, forward linkages refer to the interconnection of a firm or an industry to other firms or industries to which it sells its outputs) in a local economy, the larger an agglomeration force. To end with, the more efficient as well as the greater the nature and the scale of transportation investment, the larger an agglomeration force.

Such an interplay of the aforementioned factors is, however, indeterminate. It is therefore impossible to predict an outcome by means of an exclusive theoretical expectation. A policy implication from the same is that an impact of an improved transportation system on a regional economy is context-specific, and must be assessed on a case-by-case basis.

An emphasis on visible externalities may be less relevant to an advanced economy, where invisible externalities are more pronounced. Such an emphasis is, however, functional in comprehending an industrial clustering in a developing economy as well as for making a case for an infrastructural investment in an underdeveloped economy – and certainly for the relatively much underdeveloped state of Nagaland, where tangible externalities argument is relevant, and where transportation cost is certainly a determining factor. For a discussion on the expected socio-economic gains from connectivity improvement in Nagaland, see Humtsoe (2020).

Transportation as Additional Factor of Production

A transportation infrastructure enters the production process as a direct input (Pradhan and Bagchi, 2013). Transport per se can be therefore arguably viewed as a factor of production in itself, and can be incorporated as such in a production function. An econometric modelling on transport and growth proceeds likewise. Employing the Cobb-Douglas production function again:

$$Q_t = Ae^{rt} K_t^{a1} L_t^{a2} E_t^{a3} T^{a4} O_t^{a5},$$

where Q is the output; K, L, E and O are capital, labour, energy and other resources respectively, with T as a transport input; A, a1, a2, a3, a4, a5 and r are all constants; and t is the current year.

Rewriting the function in terms of a growth rate:

$$Q'/Q = r + a_1 K'/K + a_2 L'/L + a_3 E'/E + a_4 T'/T + a_5 O'/O$$

In the above equation, with an increase in T'/T (an increase in transport input), Q'/Q rises by more than the increase in T'/T, for an upsurge in T'/T also makes $r > 0$. $r > 0$ captures positive externalities (such as technological and knowledge diffusion potential) that growth in T'/T occasions. In a Neoclassical framework of growth, $r > 0$ is regarded as exogenous, solely accounting for an increase in T input. In the more recent endogenous growth model, $r > 0$ is also regarded as endogenously determined within the model.

Transportation and Environment

In the production of transportation services, a pecuniary cost as well as a non-pecuniary cost are involved. The concern of the present section is, however, limited to environmental cost – still commonly regarded as of a nature of non-pecuniary social cost (a cost borne by society as a whole). Although the praxis of internalizing externalities (converting non-pecuniary cost into pecuniary cost – say, by making the polluters pay for the pollution) is still at the nascent stage, the theory of monetary valuation of externalities is now well-developed. For a discussion on valuation of externalities, see Hayden (1989), Atkinson and Mourato (2008) and Legesse et al. (2022). In spite of being an indispensable component of an economic activity (as discussed earlier), transport nevertheless engenders a number of negative environmental impacts. Such environmental bads can be broadly categorized into *pollution* and *land-take* in terms of geographical extent of impact as well as temporal incidence of impact (Tietenberg, 2003; Button, 2010), and are discussed in the following.

Pollution

In terms of a scale of impact, the category of pollution can be further divided into the following sub-categories. At the outset, *local pollution* including vehicular emissions (such as SO_2, CO_2 and PM_{10}) that pollute a city's ambient air, environmentally unsafe disposal of obsolete cars that pollute soil and water, traffic noise,[3] and so on. Next, *regional pollution* comprising pollutants from mobile traffic source (such as SO_2 and NO_2) that causes acid rain, maritime spillage from oil tankers, and so on. Finally, *global pollution* including vehicular emissions of carbon dioxide (CO_2) and chlorofluorocarbons (CFCs) that causes global warming and ozone depletion respectively.

Such a non-pecuniary nature of cost – arising from the aforesaid category of pollution – is notably not of the nature of opportunity cost (the forgone value of the next best alternative use of a resource), but is incurred in the form of a *by-product* that accompanies the production process of transport infrastructure (say, in the manufacture of vehicles) as well as services (say, in the provision of logistic service). Such a cost therefore does not generally enter as a cost in the reckoning of a transport service producer as well as a transport service consumer, unless consciously acted so by espousing a societal and an environmental perspective. A divergence between private cost and social cost consequently arises, calling for an environmental policy intervention. Such a case of divergence within the transport sector can be illustrated by means of a private trip cost (PTC) and a social trip cost (STC).

A private trip cost, on the one hand, is a cost per commuter, and can be construed as an average cost (AC). It is a sum of monetary cost (say, ₹10 per km) and trip time times an opportunity cost. By way of an illustration, if the commuter is a worker, its trip cost will also include its trip time wage per unit time (say, an hour) – suggesting a higher trip cost with a higher trip time – besides monetary cost (say, fuel cost). A social trip cost, on the other hand, is the sum of private trip cost and external cost (say, vehicular pollution). It is associated with a marginal (additional) vehicle, and therefore can be understood as a marginal cost (MC).

An individual commutes by a private car as long as its willingness to pay for the trip (or marginal benefit) exceeds its private trip cost. It is learnt from Microeconomics that any point on a demand curve represents a willingness to pay. Accordingly, an intersection (or an equilibrium) between a demand curve and an average or private trip cost curve gives an individually optimum traffic volume and a corresponding equilibrium trip cost. Analogously, an intersection between a demand curve and a marginal or social trip cost curve gives a socially optimum traffic volume and a parallel equilibrium trip cost. By employing an average cost–marginal cost analysis (AC–MC analysis), a divergence between a private trip cost and a social trip cost, producing an externality cost, can be graphically worked out (in terms of Figure 2.1).

In Figure 2.1, while the x-axis measures the total number of vehicles per lane per hour (T), the y-axis measures AC and MC. From a private individual's

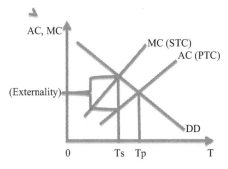

Figure 2.1 Average cost–marginal cost analysis.

standpoint, as borne out by the intersection between the demand curve, DD, and the private trip cost curve, AC (PTC), Tp number of T is an optimum. From a societal viewpoint, however, as borne out by the intersection between the demand curve, DD, and the social trip cost curve, MC (STC), Ts is an optimum, with T_s less than Tp (Ts < Tp). The said divergence arises for: while a private commuter does not consider externalities, a society considers externalities generated owing to an additional T (TsTp). That section marked as externality in the figure is an externality cost, which may need to be internalized (or removed) by bringing down T to Ts level. In conjunction with an environmental consideration, however, such a reduction in T should be affected considering developmental and welfare dimensions (as suggested in the theoretical model on congestion mitigation discussed in Chapter 4). Such a nature of comprehensive policy exercise is in accordance with an imperative of an apposite growth path – a growing economy in a salubrious environment.

Land-Take

Unlike pollution, the category of *land-take* represents an opportunity cost. A construction of a transport infrastructure (such as a roadway) engenders a social cost owing to a loss of ecosystem service (say, in the form of an aesthetic forfeiture from a defaced landscape), an islanding effect (such as a disruption to a wildlife movement corridor owing to a fragmentation of habitat) and so on (Tietenberg, 2003). Such social cost is of the nature of opportunity cost since the same involves forgoing value from alternative usage of land (or value from just how an ecosystem presently or pristinely stands).

Optimal Environmental Enhancement

From the foregoing discussion, it emerges that transport is a double-edged sword entailing benefit as well as cost. An elimination of an environmental

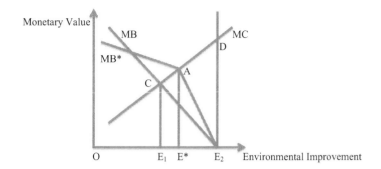

Figure 2.2 Optimal environmental enhancement.

cost attributable to transport per se entails a cost – a mitigation cost as well as an opportunity cost. 'Economists tend to, therefore, think in terms of optimizing the level of pollution rather than "purifying" the environment entirely' (Button, 2010). Adapting from Button (2010), and further developing over the same, the case of an *optimal environmental enhancement* can be graphically illustrated by means of a marginal cost–marginal benefit analysis (MC–MB analysis) as shown in Figure 2.2.

In Figure 2.2, while the vertical axis measures monetary value of cost as well as benefit from an environmental enhancement, an extent of environmental enhancement is measured along the horizontal axis. An incremental cost of environmental improvement (say, vehicular emission reduction) typically increases (if not continuously, then up to a considerable extent) with an increase in the same (say, with an installation of a cleaner combustion engine in a vehicle). The MC curve therefore slopes upwards. For most individuals, the perceived incremental benefit diminishes with a continual environmental improvement, in part because the individuals are 'likely to be relatively less conscious of lower levels of emission and be aware that many of the seriously toxic materials are likely to be among the first to be removed in the clean-up program' (Button, 2010). The MB curve therefore slopes downwards. A note may be made of the clearly anthropocentric approach being adopted in the valuation technique of the nature in practice – expressly, the *cost and benefit* to the biodiversity at large (although extremely difficult to accurately quantify) are not considered in the said practice.

An optimal extent of environmental improvement is determined by an intersection of MC and MB curves (OE_1 in Figure 2.2), beyond which a marginal cost of a further environmental improvement exceeds a perceived marginal benefit from the same. Any improvement beyond OE_1 is therefore sub-optimal, and if extended up to OE_2, a net welfare loss[4] (equal to the area of CDE$_2$ in Figure 2.2) arises. In essence, 'when talking about the excessive environmental harm caused by various forms of transport, it is important to remember that this is an excess above the optimal level of pollution, not above zero pollution or some perceived "pure" environment' (Button, 2010).

The value (or benefit) of an environmental improvement as perceived by the people is contingent inter alia on access to information as well as economic status. In essence, the probability of perceiving a greater benefit against a given cost incurred on improving an environment correlates positively with information (say, concerning ecosystem services) and economic position – the economically more well off are comparatively more probable to consider environmental concerns (possibly with the exception of certain traditional yet green lifestyles of some ethnic groups who are seemingly poor).

In a scenario of an enhanced information and an improved economic status, the MB curve will take a shape as MB* in Figure 2.2 (as opposed to the shape of MB), with the MC curve remaining unchanged. Accordingly, the optimal extent increases to E*, with the net welfare loss constricting to ADE$_2$ in the event of an environmental improvement up to E$_2$. The same is mentioned to underscore a policy salience of information dissemination (by means of either an awareness campaign or otherwise) and the case of an economic development for an environmental enhancement.

Transportation and City

Given the immense significance of waterways in socio-economic terms in the past, it is only expected that in the history of the great civilizations of humankind (such as the Indus Valley Civilization in the Indian subcontinent, the Nile Valley Civilization in Egypt and the Yellow Huang He River Valley Civilization in China), the economic centres flourished alongside riverbanks and coastlines, where inland waterways as well as oceanic waterways supported production as well as trade. 'The growth of many of the world's greatest cities is linked to their locational advantage of being along a waterway, facilitating movement of labour and raw materials as well as shipment of products to regional, national and international markets' (Mohanty, 2014). Overseas in the United States (US), Krugman (2010) noted the following concerning the growth of the New York City, 'there has been no important commercial traffic on the Erie Canal since 1850, yet the head start that the canal gave to New York City has allowed New York to remain the largest US city to this day.' Over here in Modern India, 'Thorton's famous chart of the Hooghly River [presents] a map of the plentiful towns and trading settlements along the lower Ganges' (Sen, 2021). Here in the state of Nagaland, the commercial city of the state, Dimapur, flourished as *the city near the great river*, the Dhansari River.

With an advancement in non-waterways of transportation, cities with no advantages of waterways also sprang up (Mohanty, 2014). Mass transit railways, for instance, played a significant role in the making of cities through-out the world (Government of New Zealand, 2014). Accordingly,

> Nagaland has only one railhead and one airport, both located in Dimapur city. All essential commodities come into Nagaland and to the neighbour-ing [state of] Manipur through Dimapur railhead. And given the connectiv-ity advantage, Dimapur city is [a] main commercial hub in NER.
>
> (Humtsoe, 2022)

Such a synergetic relationship between transport and urban agglomeration is discussed further in the following.

A consideration of transport cost influences where a firm locates, and thereby influences the growth of a city. 'Transport cost savings can be viewed as a type of pecuniary agglomeration effect, which may draw firms to a large city when both its market and suppliers are located there' (Brueckner, 2011). For most firms, the interaction between scale economies and transport cost governs the choice of modes between centralized pro-duction and dispersed production. A centralized production (say, in a large city) is chosen if – in the reckoning of a firm – the sum of the transporta-tion cost and production cost in such an arrangement is relatively lesser in comparison to a dispersed production in multiple regions. In other words, the former

> will be favoured when scale economies are strong and transport cost are low . . . since strong scale economies lead to a substantial production-cost saving advantage for centralized production, while low transport costs mean that this advantage isn't offset by the cost of shipping out the output.
>
> (Brueckner, 2011)

Depending on whether the nature of production is either a weight-losing or a weight-gaining process, the consideration of transportation cost inter alia determines the location of production centres. In terms of shipping cost, it is cost-efficient to locate near a market in the case of a weight-gaining production process, and to locate near a source of raw material in the case of a weight-losing production process. The centres of employment are where firms are located, and accordingly wherever the firms are located are where workers move in. In such a way, the cost of shipping influences the formation as well as the expansion of a city. The ongoing globalization of a scale never observed before is made possible and continues to be driven by a continu-ally advancing transportation (and communication) system, which presents 'unique opportunities to cities to benefit from scale and network economies' (Mohanty, 2014).

Transport is not only of prime salience in the formation of a city, but also of an equal significance in the running of a city:

> Transportation is an input to all urban activities. A good network of roads, coupled with an efficient mass transportation system, contributes to the working efficiency of cities. Household benefit from [an enhanced] public transportation through a reduction in commuting cost and travel time, expansion in housing opportunities, and increase in accessibility to employment, education, healthcare, shopping, and recreation. Firms benefit from access to new markets, specialized inputs, knowledge spillovers, skilled labour pool, cheaper and more reliable freight services, and decreased inventories to 'just in time' levels . . . New Growth theory suggest that better transportation leads to larger factor productivity by facilitating human capital externalities in cities.
>
> (Mohanty, 2014)

Urban Mobility and Urban Land Use

Historically, urban transportation system is a factor of significance that shapes the pattern of land use in an urban space. The earliest work on the problem of land allocation to alternative uses is probably Von Thunen's land rent model – explaining agricultural land rent differential in an otherwise homogenous space. A transportation cost saving, according to the said model, accounts for such a land rent differential – with higher rent for lower transportation cost, and vice versa. The said conception of Von Thunen was applied by Haig (1926) in an urban context, and further advanced that 'site rentals are charges which can be made for sites where accessibility may be had with comparatively low transportation cost.' Site rentals form a part of the price mechanism that brings about a locational equilibrium (a situation where there is no incentive either for a firm or for a household to change a current location), wherein, ceteris paribus, the highest bidder (by outbidding other rivals) gains an ownership of the most accessible land. Accessibility cost, in such a way, partly determines land-use pattern.

A city of the past (or in an initial stage) tends to be mono-centric or exhibits a 'concentric pattern of development around the main rail terminal (or occasionally port) . . . [for] local distributional services evolved much more slowly' (Button, 2010). A stylized illustration of a spatially mono-centric city, adapted from Button (2010), is shown in Figure 2.3. A city of today is multi-centric with employment centres spreading across a city. In order to underscore the function of transportation cost in the determination of the spatial shape of a city, however, the given simplified illustration suffices.

The wealthy, possessing willingness as well as ability to pay for any mode of mobility (and a large plot of land), reside in the outer rings of a city. An

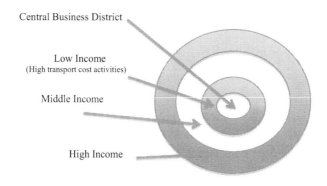

Central Business District

Low Income
(High transport cost activities)

Middle Income

High Income

Figure 2.3 Mono-centric city.

industry and commerce, for which the trade-off between site rent and transportation cost works out to be more profitable in locating at the city core or within the inner rings (say, owing to agglomeration economies, and thereby greater revenue potential), bids higher and locate accordingly. The poorer people (incapable of paying a high transportation cost) as well as others (with a low preference for a large site for an economic reason or otherwise) bid higher for smaller sites and locate accordingly in the inner areas. What then emerges of an urban land use is the form depicted in Figure 2.3.

The gradual advancement in transportation system (and the availability of the same) influences the spatial form and shape that a city gradually develops. 'The introduction of motorized public transport (initially the tramcar and later omnibus) followed by the motor car encouraged the growth of an axial pattern of urban land use . . . in ribbon development along the main road arteries' (Button, 2010). At present, 'the widespread adoption of the automobile, combined with improved road system, has [accordingly] led to the growth of multi-nucleus cities where there are numerous sub-centres and suburbs' (Button, 2010).

As already mentioned, modern cities are multi-centric, with some enormously large in terms of a geographical spread. For reasons of agglomeration economies, retails of similar nature (in terms of products sold), related firms (in terms of raw materials, intermediate inputs, social overhead or finished products) and households (sharing certain common attributes such as income and culture) cluster in distinct locations, engendering a spatially segregated city. Along with such an organically evolving spatial segregation, an urban planning authority also resorts to zoning of a city into residential, commercial, industrial and suchlike zones. For health as well as environmental rationales, furthermore, certain industries (and thereby employment centres) are altogether legally required to locate certain distance away from a city. Centres of employment and residence are therefore spread across such a consequent multi-nucleus city, extending even to a suburb. All this has necessitated a long-distance intra-city (and even an inter-city) as well as a reverse commuting (commuting outwards to a suburb for work), as opposed to commuting inwards to the core of a city. In the light of all this, the increasingly prime importance of urban transport cannot be overemphasized.

For any city to be a green engine of growth, a sustainable urban mobility is imperative. In the absence of the same, an economically productive, a socially inclusive and an environmentally sustainable city – which is well positioned to meet the existing as well as the emerging urban challenges – will not actualize. Instead, an enormous economic cost owing to traffic congestion and such-like inefficiencies (causing a higher monetary as well as a non-monetary cost of mobility) as well as an enormous environmental cost (and the consequent health-related cost) owing to a vehicular pollution will be incurred. A green urban mobility is therefore indispensable in order to minimize the sector's contribution to environmental cost, and to maximize the sector's contribution to economic growth. Creating such a mobility system entails inter alia an integrated transport–land use policy.

Integrated Transportation–Land Use Policy

As can be understood from the preceding discussion, a bidirectional relationship exists between transportation and space use. While a consideration of mobility cost influences the locational decision of a household as well as a firm, the same decision necessitates either a longer or a shorter mobility necessity. Such a relationship is encapsulated in the conceptualization of *land use–transport feedback cycle*, which posits that:

> (1) Distribution of land uses in a region determine the location of human activities such as living, working, shopping, education, or leisure; (2) Geographic spread of human activities calls for trips in the transport system to overcome the physical distance between activity locations; (3) Distribution of infrastructure in the transport system creates opportunities for spatial interactions measured by accessibility; and (4) Differential accessibility co-determines location decisions and results in changes in the land use system.
> (Geurs and Wee, 2004)

Given such a feedback cycle, land-use planning should not be carried out sans an accompanying transportation planning, and vice versa. It is essential to consider the probable differential land-use effects while assessing economic as well as environmental impacts of a major mobility project. Accordingly, effecting a major alteration in an existing urban transport system to bring about a sustainable mobility often entails a change in land use. An integration of the binary is therefore called for.

For the rapidly urbanizing developing economies,

> transportation-land use integration is perhaps the single-most important policy tool available to planners . . . to promote orderly urban development. It enhances efficiency, productivity, and the liveability of cities. . . . However, [it] can be used effectively only in a flexible planning framework as opposed to rigid master planning.
>
> (Mohanty, 2014)

For the growing unplanned cities in the developing countries, such a policy assumes an even more salience. Empirical evidences from South Korea and Japan 'suggest that the larger the city, the more important it is to invest in public transit and to integrate land use and transportation' (Mohanty, 2014).

City and Economic Growth

Economic growth – to begin with, in the form of an agricultural surplus in a rural economy – contributes to an emergence and expansion of a city (with the agricultural surplus of the ruralites feeding the urbanites, to begin with), with the latter further feeding into the former by acting as an engine of growth, resulting in a cycle of cumulative causation. The theoretical underpinnings of an urban agglomeration as an engine of growth are discussed in Chapter 3. It is comprehended from New Economic Geography (as well as theory of agglomeration economies) that an additional productivity gain arising from an agglomeration of households and firms acts as a centripetal force, causing a cumulative process of clustering. Certain positive externalities can emanate only when economic entities spatially cluster in close proximity. Notwithstanding the ongoing information technology (IT) revolution, knowledge flow, for instance, does not always occur sans space but 'is embedded in the routines of firms, people and institutions' (Mohanty, 2014).

City and Environment

Any economic entity interacts directly and indirectly with the systems of an environment. A city, as a distinct economic entity, is no exception. In actuality, the ecological footprint of cities, individually as well as entirely, is considerable; and with the ongoing rapidly paced urbanization, it is only increasing at an exponential rate. Urbanites have a greater consumption pattern than ruralites since 'increased consumption is a function of urban labour markets, wages [income], and household structure' (Torrey, 2004) and urban lifestyle.

The burgeoning urban population is adversely impacting all the components of an environment by means of the growing extraction and consumption of resources, and the consequent generation of by-products as well as wastes. Concerning the lithosphere component, diverse flora and fauna are being destroyed either for a city to spring up or for a city to spatially expand, and then to grow food as well as to extract resources for sustaining such a city. Regarding the atmosphere component, the growing urban consumption of extractive resources has engendered atmospheric contamination as well as global warming in an increasing measure (and the conspicuously consequent climate change).

> Such urbanization has created 'urban heat islands' where buildings and roads absorb and re-emit the sun's heat more than natural landscapes, resulting in temperatures up to 7°F higher than outlying areas and intensifying the effects of climate change, including risks to human health.
>
> (Randall, 2015)

Concerning atmosphere component furthermore and hydrosphere component, industrialization in urban agglomerations undesirably affects the weather and hydrologic patterns of a wider regional environment.

> Regions downwind from large industrial complexes . . . see increases in the amount of precipitation, air pollution, and the number of days with thunderstorms. . . . Urban areas generally generate more rain, but they reduce the infiltration of water and lower the water tables. This means that runoff occurs more rapidly with greater peak flows. Flood volumes increase, as do floods and water pollution downstream.
>
> (Torrey, 2004)

Above all, other environmental concerns attributable to unmanaged or undermanaged or mismanaged urbanization (such as insufficient potable water supply, inadequate solid waste management, industrial pollution and so on) are worsening.

All the aforesaid environmental concerns (and the consequent health concerns) are a major drain on the economy (in terms of lost workdays, cost of treatment, capital cost of cleaning up contaminants) and so on. Making a city as a green engine of growth is therefore imperative – and the same is the concern of the next chapter.

Conclusion

The interrelationship between and among different variables of interests that have been explored in the chapter can be summarized through the following stylized flowchart (Figure 2.4).

In Figure 2.4, the arrows emanating from environment, which project and touch transport, economic growth and city respectively, represent the flows

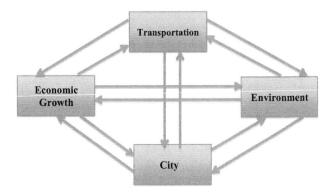

Figure 2.4 Interrelationship among variables.

from the former to the latter. The same represent the various forms in which the former is employed as input in the production of the latter. The same also therefore denotes the depletion of environmental (read as natural) resources and the associated opportunity cost. Conversely, the flows to the environment from the rest of the variables represent the production of varied environmental bads, and thereby an environmental degradation. The flows between transport and economic growth, between transport and city as well as between city and economic growth are similarly bidirectional. In perspective, while an augmentation in transportation system contributes to an economic growth, the latter also provides the necessary resources to augment the former. Analogously, a city is an engine of growth; however, without economic growth (say, in the form of an agricultural surplus in a rural economy), the former would not have come about. Still, transport plays an indispensable role in the genesis and growth of a city; however, a city by contributing to economic growth provides the required capital to invest in transport.

The interrelated nature of the relationship among the variables of interest should be appreciated in policy formulation and intervention. The notable policy implications are mentioned in the foregoing discussion in the present chapter, and the same will also inform the praxis in the context of the subject city of Kohima (discussed in later chapters). On the whole, reflecting the said interrelationship, an integrated agglomeration-transport-environment strategy is warranted.

Notes

1   A productivity enhancement refers either to an increase in the amount of output with the same quantity of input(s) or to a same amount of output with a reduced quantity of input(s).

2 The growth rate of any variable Y is denoted as Y′/Y.
3 In spite of an acoustic technological advancement of vehicle, as traffic volume and movement increase, traffic noise also increases, creating a *disamenity* effect. Such a cost is now being considered in a government compensation scheme (Tietenberg, 2003).
4 Loss of welfare can be loosely understood as loss of wellbeing.

References

Atkinson, Giles and Mourato, Susana, *Environmental cost-benefit analysis*. Annual Review of Environment and Resources, 2008. https://doi.org/10.1146/annurev.environ.33.020107.112927.

Brueckner, Jan, *Lectures in urban economics*. The MIT Press, Cambridge, MA, 2011.

Button, Kenneth, *Transport economics*. Edward Elgar Publishing Limited, The Lypiatts, UK, 2010.

Eddington, Rod, *The Eddington transport study*. Eddington, Rod, 2006. http://webarchive.nationalarchives.gov.uk/

Feiock, Richard C and Stream, Christopher, *Environmental protection versus economic development: a false trade-off?* Public Administration Review, 61(3), 2001.

Government of New Zealand, *Contribution of transport to economic development: international literature review with New Zealand perspective*. Government of New Zealand, 2014. www.transport.govt.nz/

Geurs, Karst T and Wee, Bert Van, *Accessibility evaluation of land-use and transport strategies: review and research directions*. Journal of Transport Geography 12, 127–140, 2004.

Haig, Robert Murray, *Toward an Understanding of the Metropolis: I. Some Speculations Regarding the Economic Basis of Urban Concentration*. The Quarterly Journal of Economics, vol. 40, issue 2, 179–208, 1926.

Hayden Gregory F, *Survey of methodologies for valuing externalities and public goods*. Economics Department Faculty Publications, University of Nebraska, Lincoln, 1989. https://core.ac.uk/download/pdf/188110186.pdf

Humtsoe, Tumbenthung Y, *From pathways to roadways: issues and challenges of road transport in Nagaland*. Growth and Change, 1–20, 2020. https://doi.org/10.1111/grow.12383

Humtsoe, Tumbenthung Y, *Travel mode choice in the Northeastern Indian city of Kohima: lessons from empirical study*. Journal of Urbanism: International Research on Placemaking and Urban Sustainability, 2022. DOI: 10.1080/17549175.2022.2041465

Krugman, Paul, *The new economic geography, now middle-aged*. Paper presented to the Association of American Geographers, 2010. www.princeton.edu/~pkrugman/aag

Lah, Oliver, *Sustainable urban mobility pathways: policies, institutions, and coalitions for low carbon transportation in emerging countries*. Elsevier, United Kingdom, 2018.

Legesse, Fekadu, Degefa, Sileshi and Soromessa, Teshome, *Valuation methods in ecosystem services: a meta-analysis*. Research Square, 2022. https://core.ac.uk/download/pdf/188110186.pdf

Mohanty, P K, *Cities and public policy: an urban agenda for India*. Sage, New Delhi, 2014.

Myrdal, Gunnar, *An American dilemma: the Negro problem and modern democracy*, Harper, New York, 1944.

Porter, Michael, *The competitive advantage of nations*. Free Press, New York, 1990.

Pradhan, R P and Bagchi, T P, *Effect of transportation infrastructure on economic growth in India: the VECM approach*. Research in Transportation Economics, 38(1), 139–148, 2013. https://doi.org/10.1016/j.retrec.2012.05.008

Rajagopalan, R, *Environmental studies: from crisis to cure*. Oxford University Press, New Delhi, 2011.

Randall, Cassidy, *What cities are doing to fight climate change?* National Geographic Creative Works, 2015. www.nationalgeographic.com/environment/slideshow/paid-content-what-cities-are-doing-to-fight-climate-change?fbclid=IwAR1aJYyqTiF-x9uAhA4P-NF33cOA2AVeZM_rNdFVD9GlfwXRl08e0QH0Wec

Sen, Amartya, *Home in the world: a memoir*. Allen Lane, United Kingdom, 2021.

Sinha, K R and Nongpluh, C L, *Development versus environment*. IOSR Journal of Humanities and Social Science (IOSR-JHSS), 19(8), 52–54, 2014.

Standing Advisory Committee on Trunk Road Appraisal (SACTRA) of Government of United Kingdom, *Transport and the economy report*. Government of United Kingdom, 1999. www.webarchive.nationalarchives.gov.uk/

Templet, Paul H, *The positive relationship between jobs, environment, and the economy: an empirical analysis and review*. Spectrum, 1, 37–49, 1995.

Tietenberg, Tom, *Environmental and natural resource economics*. Addison Wesley, Boston and London, 2003.

Torrey, Barbara Boyle, *Urbanization: an environmental force to be reckoned with*. Torrey, Barbara Boyle, 2004. www.prb.org/Publications/Articles/

United Nations, *New urban agenda*. United Nations, 2016. http://habitat3.org/

3 Urbanization as Green Resource

Introduction

Urbanization is justifiably the buzzword today, and it is here to stay as a phenomenon and in terms of a policy discourse. Especially in developing economies, urban spaces are rapidly sprouting as well as enlarging. Accordingly, as Mohanty (2014) opines, the 21st century will witness an urban revolution sweeping across the developing countries. It undoubtedly presents not only a policy challenge but also an opportunity to leverage the same for socioeconomic development. Urbanization is therefore the single most important policy concern for national, state and local governments in developing economies (Mohanty, 2014).

For long, studies on urbanization in developing countries forwarded the views of an *over-urbanization*, a *hyper-urbanization* or an *urban-hypertrophy*. All this, in essence, contended that the ongoing urbanization in developing economies is outpacing the going industrialization in the same, and therefore the rate of urbanization in relation to that of national income is *excessive* when compared to the experiences of developed nations. The cities in such developing countries are therefore cramped by too many migrants pushed off from agriculture queuing for industrial jobs while seeking shelter in slums. Furthermore, the *urban bias theory* suggests a biased government policy in favour of politically more powerful cities (and against the favour of semi-urban as well as rural spaces). All this portrayed a somewhat negative view of urbanization in such economies.

The aforesaid view is, however, increasingly substituted by an emerging view which sees the ongoing urbanization as an opportunity, while emphasizing the necessity to mitigate the accompanying urbanization challenges. Such a view contends that an over-urbanization argument (and suchlike views) is a fallacy, primarily for the reason that the latter argument ignores the many benefits that accrue from agglomeration (as briefed in the following). As opposed to urban bias theory, furthermore, the precarious state of cities in developing countries indicates an *anti-urban bias* in policies.

Leveraging the rapidly occurring urbanization as a resource by means of an agglomeration economies augmenting, a congestion diseconomies mitigating

DOI: 10.4324/9781032711799-5

and a resource generating city will generate a significant opportunity for economic growth. For the same, comprehending the theoretical expectations as well as exploring the empirical evidence of the gains from the going phenomenon is imperative.

Economics of Urban Agglomeration

How does an urban space, in general, come about? The following conditions must precede for such a space to come about and flourish. To begin with, an agricultural surplus (specifically, a food surplus) should arise from a rural area to provide for the urbanites. Next, the urbanites must produce certain products to exchange for agricultural surplus (food, for instance) from the ruralites. To end with, a transportation system should be in place to make the exchange possible between the spatially segregated rural and urban spaces (O'Sullivan, 2009). The emergence of a city was therefore made possible about 7000 years ago after the emergence of an agricultural surplus (Bairoch, 1988).

Historically, factors including locational advantages (such as access to waterways, natural resources or suitable climate) – collectively referred to as *first nature geography*, defence rationales and political patronage played a central role in the evolution of cities. Such exogenous factors related to geography and historical events, however, cannot wholly explain the growth of cities. Apart from such, a 'spatial organization of economic activities [in cities] also made good economic sense' (Mohanty, 2014).

The comprehension of economic rationale of a spatial organization of economic activities in an urban agglomeration – the multifarious positive externalities of agglomeration – can be appreciated by means of a metaphorical inverted pyramidal frame, beginning with the spatial organization of production under a singular roof, and then in an industrial district and finally in an urban agglomeration. As can be seen from Figure 3.1, such agglomeration economies – collectively referred to as *second nature geography* – are categorized as *internal economies of scale* (at a firm level), *localization economies* (at an industry[1] level) and *urbanization economies* (at a city level); and are enunciated in the following, beginning with the theory of a firm.

Theory of Firm

A firm is, at the outset, a specific nature of a group activity engaged in production. Spatially, such a firm can be either a *scattered* form of organizing production or an *integrated* form. An outsourcing of production to guilds is – as in the *putting out system* – an example of the former form. An avoidable cost is involved in such a scattered nature of production that can be avoided in an integrated nature. By integrating such a group activity under a singular roof, an entrepreneur commands not only a greater control over the production

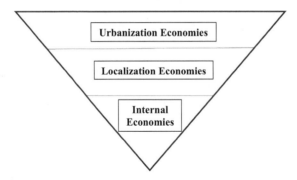

Figure 3.1 Rationales for spatial organization of economic activities.

process as well as the product but also an eliminable cost associated with collecting (from spatially scattered producers) and transporting the final product to a common market is eliminated. Such analogous internal economies of scale are further discussed in the following.

On the one hand, according to Weber (1947), a firm – as a group activity – not only occasions an *imperatively coordinated group*, but also contributes in solving the problem of uncertainty as well as the consequent need of forecasting as to what, how and for whom to produce – with such a role being undertaken by a special class of entrepreneurs. One the other hand, according to Coase (1937) and Williamson (1985), a firm – again, as a group activity – reduces *transaction cost* by reducing the necessity to negotiate and conclude an extremely asset specificity (the specific or unique characteristics of a product that is exchanged) as well as recurrent nature of contracts.

Another rationale of organizing production as a group activity is the acclaimed argument of Smith's (1776) *division of labour*. An increased productivity from a division of labour is greatly facilitated and enhanced when workers are brought together and coordinated by way of an organization. A worker, after a division of labour, specializes in and repeatedly engages in a particular operation, and thereby not only experiences an increase in dexterity, but is also facilitated to come up with certain innovations including tools that are better suited to the specific operation. A worker is furthermore enabled to save time previously lost in moving from an operation (in a certain place) to another (in a different place).

We observe in Marx's (1887) exposition on group activity the possibility of enhancing productivity by means of *cooperation*. The hitherto independent and individual workers, when brought together under a singular roof, become *social labours*, bringing forth varied positive gains. With cooperation, differences in individual capabilities are adjusted, and thereby causing a fixed minimum efficiency to each social labour. The means of production are now consumed in common on a larger scale than hitherto. The various parts of a work previously done step-wise, now progress simultaneously, and thereby churning out more output. Such a cooperation also occasions emulation and raises animal spirit (or simply, exuberance) of the workers, and thereby ushering in an increasing return. Above all, what is most striking is that the workers independently cannot produce what can be produced collectively. In perspective, the combined working day of social workers produces either a greater quantity of output or – in certain cases – an outcome that would be simply impossible if carried out individually in an equal sum of isolated working days as independent workers (a case of the phrase, the whole is greater than the sum of parts).

Theory of Industrial District

Regarding the gains from co-location of related firms, Marshall's (1890) *industrial district argument* remains a classic:

> So great are the advantages which people following the same skills trade get from near neighbourhood to one another. The mysteries of the trade become no mysteries; but as it were in the air. . . . Good work is rightly appreciated; inventions and improvements in machinery, in processes and the general organization of the business have their merits promptly discussed: if one man starts a new idea, it is taken up by others and combined with the suggestions of their own; and thus it becomes the source of further new ideas . . . subsidiary trades grow up in the neighbourhood, supplying it with implements and materials, organizing its traffic, and in many ways.

He further adds on the supply side,

> [A] localized industry gains a great advantage from the fact that it offers a constant market for skill. Employers are apt to resort to any new place where they are likely to find a good choice of workers with special skill which they require; while men seeking employment naturally go to places where there are many employers who need such skills as theirs and where therefore it is likely to find good market. [All this occasioning a case of job matching].

On the consumption side, Marshall rightly observes,

> There is also the convenience of the customer to be considered. He will go to the nearest shop for a trifling purchase; but for an important purchase he will take the trouble of visiting any part of the town where he knows that there are specialty good shops for his purpose. Consequently, shops which deal in expensive and choice tend to congregate together; and those which supply domestic needs do not. [All this suggesting the advantage of comparison shopping].

Theory of Urban Agglomeration

A discussion on a theory of urban agglomeration is incomplete sans referring to New Economic Geography (hereafter NEG). NEG brings insights from Geography into Economics, emphasizing that the former can occasion intriguingly novel insights when applied to the latter. In essence, NEG establishes that a spatial dimension of an economy is connected to an economic principle in operation in an economy (as explicated in the following).

According to NEG model, a geographical structure of an economy is the result of an interplay between a force of agglomeration (or centripetal force) and that of dispersion (or centrifugal force). In the case of producers, an agglomeration force may push firms either to co-locate in order to obtain a Marshallian trinity or 'to locate their activities in regions with bigger markets to be able to serve more consumers or where, through concentration of suppliers, the firm's input costs are lower than otherwise' (Government of New Zealand, 2014). (Named after a British economist, Alfred Marshall, Marshallian trinity refers to a trinity of rationales as to why firms in a same industry co-locate. At the outset, such firms operate in a location where a sufficient access to a rich pool of labour exists. Next, a cluster of firms in a particular location allows suppliers to specialise and achieve economies of scale, and thereby occasioning a lower cost of supply. Finally, knowledge – including new ideas – spread across firms that are located in a same region. All this enhances the productivity of the co-located firms.) In the case of consumers, an agglomeration force may similarly push households to co-locate in a larger agglomeration centre (such as to reap the benefits of comparison shopping as well as more and better job opportunities).

Furthermore, Urban Economics suggests that the many gains from an *integrated* organization of economic activities cause a denser habitation. Spatial proximity, contiguity and density stimulate 'efficiency in manufacturing, commerce and administration, which would have been impossible in a dispersed pattern of settlements. . . . It is primarily economic forces that made cities grow, stagnate or decline' (Mohanty, 2014). As Porter (1990) observes, 'successful firms concentrate in particular cities or states within a nation,' for, as Jacob (1985) opines, 'knowledge transfers occur between rather than within industries, and this transfer facilitates search and experimentation that is at the heart of innovation.' A greater diversity of economic activities in a city facilitates a greater knowledge exchange across individuals as well as enterprises.

Operating against the aforesaid centripetal force is a centrifugal force. After a certain threshold, an agglomeration also brings with it diseconomies (such as an increasing cost of land as well as labour which is observed in cities across the world, and a traffic congestion in increasingly many a city). Such an increase in cost associated with diseconomies as well as a dispersed availability of natural resources act as a dispersing force. While a certain section of people who cannot cope with such an increasing cost is pushed out (or marginalized) to the periphery of a city (such as a slum or a poor people's colony on the periphery of a city), such an increasing cost also restrict certain section of people from moving into a city.

With an integrated urban planning of the nature advanced in the book, while agglomeration diseconomies can be minimized, agglomeration economies can be maximized, and thereby making urbanization as a resource that can be leveraged.

Urbanization as Resource: Theoretical Underpinnings

The comprehension of economic rationale for spatial organization of economic activities in an urban agglomeration is critical to counter negative notions of urbanization (of the nature mentioned earlier) as well as to appreciate and leverage the same as a *green resource* for sustainable development.

To begin with, a city presents the following natures of basic gains: economies of density, scale, association and extension. At the outset, density engenders a reduction in the cost of interacting, learning, organizing, producing, transporting, consuming and so on – and thereby brings about economies of density (or simply, advantages accruing from density). It is more cost-efficient, for instance, to provide myriad social welfare services to dense settlements than to scattered smaller settlements. Next, the prospect of a greater volume of any economic opportunity in a city occasions economies of scale, which spread overhead cost[2] (as well as potential economic or investment risk) over a large number of agents. A profitable installation of a cold storage by marginal vendors collectively (or by an authority for use by the same) in order to cater to a substantial urban market, otherwise economically unfeasible when installed independently by an individual vendor (or when installed for a much smaller rural market), is an example of the same. Then, the potential of a more extensive collaboration (such as in devising joint business strategies and undertaking innovations) engenders economies of association. Finally, the greater possibility of sharing the emerging industry's optimum practices and suchlike within a city as well as between cities causes extension economies.

Urban agglomerations are subjected to the aforesaid agglomeration externalities as well as networking externalities. Such externalities

> carve out a unique role for cities as the drivers of knowledge-led growth. They facilitate knowledge externalities, with faster generation, transmission, diffusion and accumulation of knowledge, catalysing innovation. They magnify the effects of growth drivers outside the market mechanism . . . They [agglomeration externalities and networking externalities], in conjunction with market forces and public policies, benefit many actors in the spatial economy.
>
> (Panda et al., 2020)

All this makes a city a storehouse of skill as well as capital, a centre of knowledge as well as innovation, a source of formal as well as informal employment for rural–urban migrants, a substantial market for goods as well as services and a generator of resource for socio-economic development including rural development. Nagaland Vision 2030 document of the Government of Nagaland (2016) affirms that

> in the present century the urban areas are emerging as the 'engines of economic growth' as agglomeration and densification of economic activities stimulate accelerated economic growth and better opportunities. They are not only strategic centres of economic activity and living, but they are also critical for achieving inclusive growth as they provide ample social and economic opportunities.

Urbanization as Resource: Empirical Evidence

The appreciation of the advantages of urbanization goes back to the time of the Ancient Greeks. In the work, *Cyropaedia*, Xenophon (a student of the great philosopher, Socrates) 'tells of the advantage accruing to a large, as opposed to [a] small, city in the opportunity for specialization by trade – for division of labour' (Galbraith, 1991). Urbanization is historically associated with an economic as well as a social transformation, which the *World Urbanization Prospects* of the United Nations (2015) captures in the following quote:

> The process of urbanization . . . brought greater geographic mobility, lower fertility, longer life expectancy and population aging. Cities are important drivers of development and poverty reduction in both rural and urban areas . . . urban living is often associated with higher rate of literacy and education, better health, greater access to social services, and enhanced opportunities for cultural and political participation.

Numbers attest to the economic significance of a city as well. Urban-based economic activities account for up to 55% of Gross Domestic Product (GDP) in low-income countries, 73% in middle-income countries, and 85% in high-income countries (Mohanty, 2014). According to an analysis of Mckinsey Global Institute (2010), Indian cities accounted for 58% of the country's GDP in 2008, and are projected to account for nearly 70% by 2030.

Empirical studies on agglomeration economies adopt in the main the following broad approaches:

> The first, the dartboard approach, tries to demonstrate that productive activities are much more clustered than would be the case if industrial

location were based on pure random chance or comparative advantage due to spatial factors. The second approach links higher wages and land rents in larger agglomerations vis-à-vis smaller areas to their productivity differentials. The third, most popular in empirical research, aims at establishing systematic variations in productivity between larger cities and smaller towns.

(Mohanty, 2014)

Some empirical findings on agglomeration economies from both developed as well as developing economies are cited in Table 3.1.

Table 3.1 Empirical findings on agglomeration economies

Studies' Authors	Findings
	Developed Economies
Sveikauskas (1975)	In the United States (US), a doubling of an extent of a city raises labour productivity in an average manufacturing industry by 6 to 7%.
Segal (1976)	In the US, labour productivity is 8% higher in metros with a population of more than 2 million than in the remaining metros.
Glaeser and Mare (2001)	In the US, earning in metropolitans is about 28% more than that in non-urban areas.
Combes et al. (2009)	In France, firms in large cities are about 9% more productive than the firms in small cities.
Mare and Graham (2009)	In New Zealand, a doubling of an extent of a city increases output by almost 7%.
Tabuchi (1986)	In Japan, an effect of an extent of a city on manufacturing productivity ranges from 3% to 4%.
Tabuchi and Yoshida (2000)	In Japan, a doubling of an extent of a city is associated with a 10% higher nominal wage.
Henderson et al. (2001)	In Korea, localization economies exist in 23 industries located in metropolitans.
	Developing Economies
World Bank (2006)	In China, a survey of firms in cities suggests that firms in a more populated city are more productive.
Diechmann et al. (2007)	In Indonesia, a strong influence of existing firms in a city as well as localization economies are evident in a plant location choice.
Shukla (1984)	In India, resource utilization in a city with a population of 100,000 is about 23% more efficient than that in a city with a population of 10,000. It is as much as 51% more efficient in a city with a population of a million than that in a city with a population of 10,000.

Source: Adapted from Mohanty (2014)

Urbanization as Green Resource

It may appear reasonable to assume that environmental bads (and the consequent economic cost) proliferate with an increase in the spatial extent of a city.
On the contrary, however,

> many of the effects of urban areas on the environment are not necessar-
> ily linear. Bigger urban areas do not always create more environmental
> problems. And small urban areas can cause large problems. Much of what
> determines the extent of the environmental impacts is how the urban popu-
> lations behave – their consumption and living patterns – not just how large
> they are.
>
> (Torrey, 2014)

An urban agglomeration can, in contrast, contribute to an environmental
enhancement by augmenting sustainable economic growth (as discussed
earlier), and thereby enhancing resources for restoration of environmental
degradation as well as for preservation of the same. Bringing about such
a contribution requires development and management strategy of a city
informed by growth as well as environmental considerations, and good urban
governance to implement the same.

Citing the requirement of economic growth as well as the obligation for
social justice (say, employment for all), the historic tendency of humankind evidentially places development in general and development of a city
in particular above environmental concerns. A received notion is therefore
that urbanization typically degrades an environment. As opposed to the said
notion, however, a city can be constructive for an environment – qualified by
the phrase, *if managed appositely* – for the following rationales.

To begin with, a city (as expounded earlier) contributes to a higher productivity owing to economies arising out of an agglomeration as well as scale.
It implies that either more or the same amount of output can be produced by
employing smaller amount of input with urbanization than without. For the
same reason, an environmentally friendly public infrastructure is much more
economical to construct, maintain and operate in a dense urban space than in
a sparse rural space. Analogously, since density is an important determinant
of energy use, a city of a greater density, if not negated by traffic congestion,
reduces the distance of required trips (while also making walking, cycling and
suchlike non-motorized modes of green mobility more viable), and thereby
reduces an energy use. As already discussed, an urban agglomeration facilitates innovation including green technology, which makes a *green economy*
possible. Additionally, a city generates revenue that funds research and development on green technology as well as green infrastructure projects, which
reduce the generation of environmental bads (and thereby improving public
health as well). As a final consideration, a higher standard of living associated

with urbanization can foster a pro-environment position, as mentioned earlier (Wan, 2012). Above all, considering the emerging urban environmental statistics (stated later), suggestions of the following nature may be actualized for making a city a sustainable engine of growth.

At the outset, energy efficiency as well as conservation should be enhanced by means of an appropriate pricing, regulation, public sector investment, and other suchlike means. Such an enhancement is imperative given that 'cities account for 70 % of energy consumption and 40 to 50 % of greenhouse gas emissions globally' (Randall, 2015).

An apposite pricing is essential not only to entirely account for social cost and benefit (and thereby suitably affecting the behaviour of an economic agent), but also to ensure an efficient allocation of resources. The consequent higher prices of certain environmentally damaging products (say, petroleum products) after accounting for social cost (say, cost of pollution from production and consumption of petroleum products) may induce a more judicious consumption behaviour (and thereby, reduced consumption) of the same (and thereby, reduced pollution from the same). Analogously, such resultant higher prices of ecologically degrading products (say, conventional energy) after accounting for social cost may make an allocation of resource (or investment) profitable in green technology (say, to harness unconventional energy) for the price of unconventional energy becomes competitive with the price of conventional energy (and for other suchlike business rationales). Market-based instruments (such as congestion and emission charges, carbon tax, removing inefficient subsidies, introducing or increasing block pricing – for water, electricity and other public utilities) may be therefore employed to achieve a correct pricing.

An appropriate as well as a timely regulation (including a prescribed standard wherever necessary) should be framed in order to correct market failure on air, water, vehicular emission and so on. Market failure here refers to the inability of the market – sans regulatory intervention from government – either to check environmental degradation (say, pollution) or to engender prices which account for the social cost (say, pollution). Coupling regulation with a public sector investment, while developments of the nature of a green industrial zone and suchlike should be stimulated, developments of the sort of an urban sprawl and likewise should be effectively checked.

A quantitatively as well as qualitatively adequate PTS should be planned and timely provided – as warranted by emerging necessity – in order to improve connectivity as well as to reduce environmental pollution, and to enhance the overall quality of life in a city (Wan, 2012). A traditional pavement – covering, on an average, 30–45% of an urban space, and being heated up to 150°F in summer – results in an increased necessity for an indoor cooling. Cool paving materials – which reflect solar heat, reduce storm-water runoff and improve water quality – should therefore be explored (currently being experimented at Doha in Qatar). Given that transport accounts for 37% of emissions globally, and given that electric vehicles emit about 20% as much heat as gasoline engines, while the former should be encouraged, the latter should be discouraged (Randall, 2015).

The unconventional renewable resources and emerging green technologies should be continually adopted as well as promoted. Actions in the same direction consist of constructing a waste-to-energy plant in order to reduce pollution as well as to generate renewable energy, developing a city using renewable energy as a primary energy source, building a compact (and walkable) city centred on an efficient subway system without a much reliance on a roadway, and so on (Wan, 2012). Of the nearly 33% of the entire global energy consumption being accounted for by buildings, office appliances are accountable for 14% of energy consumed in commercial buildings. A net zero energy residential as well as office building should be therefore stimulated by means of certifying green building with either a cool roof (which stays up to 50°F to 60°F cooler than a traditional roof in peak summer months) or a living roof (because plants reflect sunlight and release moisture, surface temperature of such a roof can be 30°F to 40°F lower than a traditional roof during the day, further lowering a city wide temperature by up to 5°F), innovating green office equipment, and suchlike. Furthermore, an urban forest (encompassing all the trees in a city), which can lower temperature as well as mitigate climate change by capturing and storing CO_2 should be extended (Randall, 2015).

Creating a sustainable city (expressly, in order to achieve the social inclusion component of sustainable development) also requires supporting the urban poor by reducing disaster risk as well as by improving slum condition. While constructing affordable dwellings in a safe area for the poor as well as investing in a waste management infrastructure, climate forecast technology, and so on can achieve the former, the latter can be achieved by providing basic services as well as either granting land title or providing housing voucher to slum dwellers and suchlike (Wan, 2012).

As a final consideration, public finance as well as transparency and accountability of urban governance should be strengthened. By broadening the tax base on the revenue side, and by increasing the access of urban government to capital market – thereby lowering the provisioning cost of public infrastructure and services on the expenditure side, public finance can be enhanced. To strengthen good governance, the performance of a city government should be disclosed to the public as well as non-governmental organizations (NGOs), and schemes to incentivise a *race to the top* (say, by rewarding a city government for an achievement in an area of sustainability concern) should be effected (Wan, 2012).

Urbanization as Green Factor of Production

In accordance with the discussion so far, urbanization per se can be arguably viewed as a green resource, and can be incorporated as an additional factor of production in a production function (a variety of the same is employed in econometric studies of agglomeration economies). Again, we employ the Cobb-Douglas production function:

$$Q_t = Ae^{rt} K_t^{a1} L_t^{a2} E_t^{a3} U^{a4} O_t^{a5},$$

where Q is the output; K, L, E and O are capital, labour, energy and other resources respectively, with U as an urbanization input; A, a1, a2, a3, a4, a5 and r are all constants; and t is the current year.

Rewriting the function in terms of a growth rate:

$$Q'/Q = r + a_1 K'/K + a_2 L'/L + a_3 E'/E + a_4 U'/U + a_5 O'/O$$

In the above equation, with an increase in U'/U (growth in urbanization), Q'/Q rises by more than the increase in U'/U, because the upsurge in U'/U also makes $r > 0$. $r > 0$ captures the agglomeration, networking, knowledge and other suchlike positive as well as environmentally welcoming externalities that a growth in U'/U occasions. In a Neoclassical framework of growth, the $r > 0$ is regarded as exogenous, while accounting for only the increase in U input. In the recent endogenous growth model, $r > 0$ is also regarded as endogenously determined within the model.

Conclusion

While the economic significance of urban agglomerations is unparalleled, many of such cities of today are not without concerns and challenges, especially regarding sustainability.

> Cities are perhaps one of humanity's most complex creations, never finished, never definitive, they are like a journey that never ends. Their evolution is determined by their ascent into greatness or their descent into decline. They are the past, the present and the future.
>
> (United Nations, 2008)

In order not to negate the gains of urban agglomeration – to ensure an ascent rather than a descent – such urban challenges and concerns ought to be immediately addressed. As suggested in the present Part II and will be made so in the ensuing Part III, to affect greening of the ongoing urbanization, an integrated agglomeration-mobility-environment development strategy is essential.

The New Urban Agenda of the United Nations (UN) (2017) – intended to guide the policy approach of the UN member states towards a sustainable urbanization for the coming 20 years – represents a global consensus that *our future is urban*. The current chapter presented the theoretical expectations as well as empirical substantiation that the ongoing urbanization can be made sustainable, and thereby making our future (expressly, urban agglomerations) sustainable as well. Towards the same, an inclusive and green urban mobility is indispensable, on which the book keeps making a return.

Notes

1 An industry is a group of related firms.
2 A cost which is not directly connected to production of goods and services but is nevertheless necessary for the operation of business (such as cost of utilities) is called overhead cost.

References

Bairoch, Paul, *Cities and economic development: from the dawn of history to the present*. University of Chicago Press, Chicago, 1988.

Coase, Ronald, *The nature of the firm*. Economica, 4, 386–405, 1937.

Galbraith, John Kenneth, *A History of Economics: the Past as the Present*. Penguin Books, United Kingdom, 1987.

Government of Nagaland, *Nagaland vision 2030*. Government of Nagaland, 2016. www.nagaland.gov.in/

Government of New Zealand, *Contribution of transport to economic development: international literature review with New Zealand perspective*. Government of New Zealand, 2014. www.transport.govt.nz/

Jacobs, Jane, *Cities and the wealth of nations*. 1st Vintage Books edition. Vintage, London, 1985.

Marshall, Alfred, *Principles of economics*. Atlantic Publishers and Distributors (P) Ltd, New Delhi, 1890.

Marx, K, *The capital*. Progress Publishers, Moscow, 1887.

McKinsey Global Institute, *India's urban awakening: building inclusive cities, sustaining economic growth*. McKinsey and Company, New York, 2010.

Mohanty, P K, *Cities and public policy: an urban agenda for India*. Sage, New Delhi, 2014.

O'Sullivan, Arthur, *Urban economics*. McGraw Hill, Irvine, 2009.

Panda, Prerna, Mishra, Alok Kumar and Mishra, Shibani, *Externalities and urban infrastructure financing: a new theoretical model and lessons for smart cities in India*. International Journal of Transport Economics, xlvi(1), 51–74, 2020.

Porter, Michael, *The competitive advantage of nations*. Free Press, New York, 1990.

Randall, Cassidy, *What cities are doing to fight climate change?* National Geographic Creative Works, 2015. www.nationalgeographic.com/environment/slideshow/paid-content-what-cities-are-doing-to-fight-climate-change?fbclid=IwAR1aJYyqTiF-x9uAhA4P-NF33cOA2AVeZM_rNdFVD9GlfwXRl08e0QH0Wec

Smith, Adam, *An inquiry into the nature and causes of wealth of nations* (Fingerprint! Publishing, 1 April 2018). Prakash Books India Pvt Ltd, New Delhi, 1776.

Torrey, Barbara Boyle, *Urbanization: an environmental force to be reckoned with*. Barbara Boyle, Torrey, 2014. www.prb.org/Publications/Articles/

United Nations, *New urban agenda*. United Nations, 2017. http://habitat3.org/

United Nations, *State of the world's cities 2008/2009: harmonious cities*. Earthscan, Oxford, 2008.

United Nations, *World urbanization prospects: the 2014 revision*. United Nations, 2015. https://esa.un.org/

Wan, Guanghua, *Urbanization can be good for the environment*. Wan, Guanghua, 2012.
www.asiapathways-adbi.org/

Weber, Max, *The theory of social and economic organization*, Reprint edition, Free
Press, New York, 1947/2009.

Williamson, Olliver, *The economic institutions of capitalism: firms, markets and rela-
tional contracting*. The Free Press, New York, 1985.

Part III

Praxis

4   A Highland City
at the Frontier

Introduction

As already established in Part II of the book, the economic reality of today is such that urban agglomerations are the prime generators of the wealth of nations. Cities of today are nonetheless not without problems and challenges – of economic as well as environmental nature, especially in developing economies. As shall be comprehended in Part III, such a contrasting duality is borne out from the case of the subject city of Kohima, a highland city at the frontier; wherein, comparable to many frontier economies, an integrated agglomeration-transport-environment development strategy is conspicuously absent. The consequences of such an absence of an informed policy intervention are the myriad urban challenges confronting Kohima, in the main traffic congestion, vehicular air pollution, water scarcity and so on (as explicated later). Rapid urbanization is, however, a phenomenon in the city on the hills as well (again, as elucidated in the following).

Against such a backdrop of knowledge gap and the corollary absence of informed policy making and intervention in Kohima, a historical context as well as a spatial and socio-economic profile of the city are provided in the present chapter to set a stage for engaging in an empirical enquiry of urbanism in Kohima – which is the concern of the current part of the book. In the present part, in essence, we move from an abstraction to an everyday life, from a global context to a frontier context and from a macro level to a micro level in order to make an empirical contribution (informed by theory) towards making an urban agglomeration a green engine of growth.

Towards formulating a comprehensive, integrated as well as an effective sustainable development strategy of a city, SWOT assessment of a city is of immense utility for policy makers; expressly, as an initial study to identify the challenges and prospects of such a sustainable development. SWOT analysis of Kohima is therefore made in the current chapter to begin an empirical enquiry of the said city. Above all, an economically efficient, a socially inclusive and an environmentally sustainable urban mobility system is imperative for developing a sustainable city. Urban mobility development and management strategy for Kohima is therefore taken up in the ensuing chapters in the present part.

DOI: 10.4324/9781032711799-7

History of Urbanization

Colonial legacy contributed to the gradual evolution of what was then a quaint Kohima village into the now bustling Kohima city. As was the case with almost all Naga villages, Kohima village was strategically sited on a hilltop primarily for reasons of defence – it was more tactical to watch out for enemies and defend a village in such an overlooking vantage position. A city that evolved from such a hilltop village, Kohima sits on a ridge as a highland city.

In the history of British administration in Naga Hills,[1] Kohima occupied an important place in being an early seat of colonial administration. When Nagaland became the 16th state of the Indian Union in 1963, Kohima was made the capital of the then new state. Such an initial condition occasioned a *path dependency* of sort, with Kohima continuing to be a seat of administration. (To put it simplistically, path dependency suggests that what occurred in the past continues to occur in the present.) The same continuing to occasion a substantial market for trade and commerce owing to the consequent agglomeration of people. It is, today, an agglomeration centre of salience not only to the state but also to the entire NER.

Each of the officially recognized tribes of Nagaland traditionally occupies a distinct territorial area of the state. Accordingly, the city of Kohima is sited in the indigenous homeland of the Angamis. The Angamis therefore constitute more than half of the city's population. Being the capital of the state as well as an agglomeration centre of salience to the region, however, Kohima is a cosmopolitan city with all the Naga tribals as well as *mainland Indians*[2] in residence.

Pattern of Urbanization

Although an up-to-date statistics concerning urbanization pattern of Kohima is unavailable (since the decadal census for 2021 is still not conducted at the time of writing the book), an increasing trend – as can be gleaned from the available data – is expected to remain valid even today. While for the state as a whole, the decadal population growth rate was negative, −0.48%, the district of Kohima registered a substantial growth rate of about 21% (GoI, 2011). In 2001, Kohima district was more urbanized (with about 29% urbanization rate) as compared to the state as a whole (with about 20% urbanization rate) (GoI, 2001). In 2011, while the percentage of urban population of the district increased to about 45%, the percentage of that of the state as a whole was much lower at about 29% (GoI, 2011). Accordingly, the difference in urbanization rate between that of the district and that of the state almost doubled from 8% in 2001 to about 16% in 2011. Moreover, in 2016–2017, while the percentage of farming population in the district of Kohima was analogously about 25% (lowest among the districts of the state), the percentage of that of the state as a whole was about 55% (GoN, 2022).

Reflecting an increasing agglomeration of people in the city, furthermore, about 37% of the people were born outside the city but within the state (GoN, 2006). District Human Development Report of Kohima (GoN, 2009) accordingly observes that 'increasing urbanization of Kohima is also clear' and further attributes a duality of reasons for the same. A factor of much significance is the coming of government employees from across the state to work in the capital. In consonance to the said observation, a majority of the city's population (expressly, about 55%) was engaged in various government sector jobs in 2006 (GoN, 2006). Another factor pertains to the 'influx of rural populace in search of employment, to access better education facilities for children and better prospects for livelihood' (GoN, 2009). In agreement with the said observation again, City Development Plan of Kohima (GoN, 2006) noted that 72% of the population belonged to the earning age group of 15–55 years across all income groups. In the absence of even a singular large-scale industry in operation in the city as well as in the state, the migrants – who are not government employees – work in an informal sector consisting of in the main construction and retail.

Being a centre of administration as well as education with a comparatively larger job market, Kohima exhibits a centripetal force of agglomeration. Accordingly, the Middle Income Groups (MIGs) and High Income Groups (HIGs) showed the maximum tendency of coming into the city from other parts of Nagaland to settle down (about 37% in each case) (GoN, 2006). It reflects the pull factor of the city for the MIG and HIG, which can be attributed to its administrative and commercial salience. The coming of such groups further contributes to market development and expansion, including markets of high-income elastic retails of branded franchises, which are absent in smaller towns. It in turn creates employment opportunities and offers better wages, further accentuating the agglomeration process.

Regional Setting and Connectivity

The district of Kohima shares boundaries with the district of Dimapur in the west, with the districts of Phek and Zunheboto in the east, with the district of Peren as well as the state of Manipur in the southwest, and the district of Wokha in the north. The city of Kohima that comes under the district of Kohima is therefore strategically located as a transit route for intra-state and inter-state logistic. Unless mentioned otherwise, hereafter, Kohima expressly refers to the city and not to the district as a whole (as is being done until now without explicitly mentioning so), which includes rural as well as semi-urban areas.

Kohima possesses a reasonably adequate road connectivity with all the neighbouring states. Furthermore, it is located on the envisioned Asian Highway-1, the transnational highway, which is projected as India's gateway to Eastern Asia (and therefore forming a critical aspect of India's Act East Policy). Notably, Asian countries, in spite of possessing rich resources,

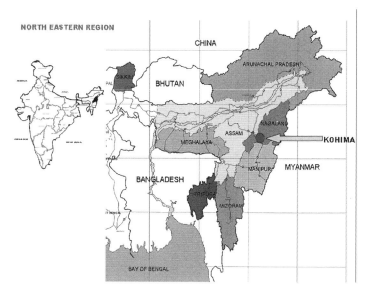

Figure 4.1 Regional setting and connectivity.
Source: GoN (2006)

fail to utilize the said potential for want of regional connectivity (Ivan Su et al., 2011). Studies have shown that countries with geographical proximity could substantially benefit from more trade provided such a cost of trading is minimized with infrastructural provision as well as institutional change. The proposed international highway is therefore a welcome development for the region, and in terms of the geographical position of Kohima, it spells the immense potential of the city to be an internationally connected agglomeration centre. Figure 4.1 gives a pictorial representation of Kohima's regional setting and connectivity.

As of 2003–2004, the percentage road length of Kohima district in the state's total was about 18% with an extent of 2367 km. More than 65% of the road in the district is surfaced as compared to the state's average of about 46%. Also, the density of surfaced road per sq. km in the district (about 50%) is much higher than the state's average (about 38%) (GoN, 2009). While such statistics indicate that the district as a whole is much better off than the other districts of the state in terms of road network and road condition, the same also suggests that the city in particular is also much better off than the other urban areas of the state in the said parameters. Above all, developmental works are currently in progress to connect Kohima with a railway to further enhance its connectivity with the rest of the country.

Physical Growth Pattern

The city of Kohima is situated on a ridge with a number of small hillocks and valleys. Several areas are steep with clifflike features that are unsuitable for habitation. Furthermore, the entire city is prone to landslide owing to its geology. Accordingly, landslide regularly occurs especially in monsoon season, and mostly on the eastern as well as western slopes of the city – causing inter alia property damages. The existing physical growth pattern is therefore determined primarily by the availability of stable land in terms of susceptibility to landslide. The current physical structure of the city can be termed as largely *linear* with growth concentrated along the major roads (GoN, 2006).

The direction of the going physical growth pattern of Kohima is also controlled by physical characteristics and accessibility (say, availability of accessible habitable lands). Accordingly, GoN (2006) projects that urban spatial growth is expected to occur mainly in the more stable northern part along the National Highway 2 (NH-2) (erstwhile NH-61). The establishment of the New Capital Complex (where the secretariat as well as other offices of the government are sited) in the northern part is also triggering such a growth in the same part. Towards the southern direction, the reserved forest, *Pulie Badze*, acts as the de facto boundary. GoN (2006) notes the following constraints of growth: cantonment area, forested areas, privately owned land under tribal control (explained in the following), landslide areas and steep slopes.

The ongoing attempt of the Urban Development Department (UDD) of the state government to develop the New Capital Complex is encountering a land acquisition problem. Notably, no land in the state can be acquired under the extant land acquisition laws in the country given the protection accorded to the tribals of the state in the Indian Constitution. As per Article 371A of the Indian Constitution, no act of Parliament in respect of Naga customary law and procedure as well as ownership and transfer of land and its resources shall apply to the State of Nagaland unless the Legislative Assembly of Nagaland by a resolution so decides. Such a provision, according to the City Development Plan of Kohima (GoN, 2006), often becomes a hindrance for further development of the city. For a further discussion on the institutional constraint to development in the state arising from a conflict of traditional and modern institutions, see Walling and Humtsoe (2021). Accordingly, the state government was able to acquire only 50% of the required land (2000 acres) for developing the New Capital Complex (GoN, 2006).

Existing Land-Use Pattern

The extant land-use pattern of Kohima is shown in Table 4.1. In 2006, while an administrative land use accounted for the highest at 45%, it was followed by a residential use at about 8%. The nature of land use within the city is that of a mixed land use, with residential buildings alongside the streets frequently

Table 4.1 Pattern of land use

Land use	Area (in ha)	Percentage
Residential	533.6	7.85
Commercial	16.83	0.25
Administrative	3065	45.07
Industrial	2.4	0.04
Recreational	3.37	0.05
Transportation	4.6	0.07
Paramilitary and police	36.7	0.54
Agricultural land use	208.63	3.07
Cremation grounds, burial grounds and water bodies	3.56	0.05
Jhum cultivation	28.6	0.42
Conservation area	2897.5	42.61
Total	6801	100.00

Source: GoN (2006)

having commercial establishments on the ground floors (GoN, 2006). Commercial buildings are generally of multi-storeys, consuming disproportionately reduced area of land. Also, vegetable vendors vend alongside the road sans a proper structure. Accordingly, while the reported percentage of residential area would be a slight overestimation, the negligible percentage of commercial use (0.25%) would be a slight underestimation.

Central Business District

While *Von Thunen's model* suggests decreasing population density as well as land rent with an increasing distance from the city centre, standard *Alonso-Muth-Mills' model* postulates that a lower commuting cost offset a higher house rent in and around a city centre. Such models can offer an explanation to the spatial spread of population in Kohima. The population density varies considerably from as low as 30 persons per sq. km up to as high as 200 persons per sq. km. Areas where commercial establishments as well as government offices are mostly concentrated are the densest areas[3] (GoN, 2006). Such denser habitations can be construed as the *Central Business Districts* (CBD) in the context of Kohima.

As is often the case in a smaller city where a *mall culture* is still undeveloped, the entire commercial area extends along the main street of the city[4] producing a more or less linear CBD. The said existing commercial area is spatially constrained for an expansion, and therefore multi-storey buildings have come up in the said area (GoN, 2006). Such a constraint may be for reasons of topography (steep slopes, for instance) as well as inconvertibility of land use (refusal of residential house owners to relocate, for instance). Notably, as per the building regulation of Urban Development Department as well as Kohima Municipal Council (KMC), the height of buildings should not exceed 49 feet (equivalent to 5 storeys) for geological rationales. An expansion of the existing CBD is therefore vertically as well as horizontally constrained.

It is apparent that congestion diseconomies have emerged along the largely linear CBD; of which, an almost immobile traffic congestion and a worsening vehicular air pollution are of immediate concerns (discussed in the ensuing chapters). It is therefore imperative to alleviate such diseconomies through an appropriate policy intervention.

State of Economy

The economy of Kohima is largely driven by service sector in the main public administration. That it is so is demonstrated not only by the administrative land use accounting for the highest land use in the city (as discussed earlier), but also by the work participation and occupational structure of the city (as discussed in the following). The same is also true for the entire state as well (see Walling and Humtsoe, 2021).

Work Participation and Occupational Structure

Although employment statistics specifically for the city of Kohima is unavailable, the number of employed people (in public sector as well as private sector) is highest in the district of Kohima in 2021, constituting about 26% of the total number of employed people in the state (GoN, 2022). As is evident from Table 4.2, a marked variation characterizes the occupational variety of the various income groups in 2006. Given the 'near absence of private sector' (Walling and Humtsoe, 2021) in the state, it can be ascertained that among the Low Income Group (LIG), MIG as well as HIG, a majority is engaged in government sector. Among the Below Poverty Line (BPL), about 45% are engaged as daily hired labourers, which provide them neither a secured source of income nor an adequate wage (and therefore, poverty). Marginally Poor Group (MPG) are engaged either in subsistence agriculture or in traditional crafts and small shops of marginal scale. The engagement of the BPL as well as the MPG in such marginal activities reflects the absence of any organized manufacturing-based jobs within the city (as discussed in the following). Such an absence continues even today, and therefore the employment profile may be more or less the same even today (although the stated statistics is related to 2006, and an updated data is unavailable).

Concerning workforce participation rate in Kohima, it declined from 35% in 1991 to 33% in 2001 (GoN, 2006). Although an exact data on Kohima City is unavailable, the proportion of workforce excluding marginal workers for the Kohima district as a whole was about 38% in 2011 (GoI, 2011), suggesting a probable increase in the same rate for Kohima as well.

Concerning the proportion of overall marginal workforce, it increased from less than 1% in 1991 to 7% in 2001; of which, the increase in female

Table 4.2 Occupational profile of different income groups (in percentage)

Income Group	Occupational Profile					
	Agriculture	Traditional Crafts	Hired Labour and Daily Wages	Own Shop/ Business	Government/ Private Sector	Others
Below Poverty Line (BPL)	25	5	45	25	0	0
Marginally Poor Group (MPG)	31.3	15.6	3.1	15.6	0	34.4
Low Income Group (LIG)	12.6	2.3	3.4	27.1	40.1	14.5
Middle Income Group (MIG)	5.2	0.9	2.1	18.3	52.6	20.9
High Income Group (HIG)	2.1	0.4	2.1	12.8	65.4	17.2
All	5.7	1.2	2.5	17.5	54.5	18.6

Source: GoN (2006)

marginal workers was notably significant – from less than 1% in 1991 to 11% in 2001. Such an increasing marginalization of labour was mainly attributed to the deficiency of adequate economic opportunities on the one hand and the absence of required skills for the prevailing deficient employment opportunities on the other hand (GoN, 2006). Again, although an exact data on Kohima is unavailable, suggesting a positive turn in the trend, the overall marginal workforce as well as the female marginal workforce declined to about 6% in 2011 (GoI, 2011).

Industry

Industry in the city of Kohima as well as in the state of Nagaland is grossly underdeveloped. The new industrial policy of the state, Nagaland State Industrial Policy, formulated in 2000 to promote an industrial development in the state, is thus far unsuccessful in enabling investors to generate substantial employment and income for the people of the state. In 2006, around 80 small-scale industrial units engaged – on an average – six to seven employees in Kohima. In 2013, while Kohima district registered the second highest number of permanent Micro, Small and Medium Enterprises (MSMEs) in the state (yet only 95 MSMEs) generating 570 employments, Dimapur district registered the highest number of permanent MSMEs (yet only 146 enterprises) generating 876 employments (GoN, 2014). All this suggests that the manufacturing sector remains stagnant in the city as well as in the state.

On the state of secondary sector in Nagaland, Walling and Humtsoe (2021) observed the following, which is also accurate for Kohima as well:

> The few entrepreneurial ventures that are there in the state exhibit elitist [tendency] of sort. In the absence of basic infrastructural and institutional support, [it] is expected. [At the outset], most of [the high income elastic] ventures are by those [who] are, to begin with, in advantaged positions, having connections and capital, [such as] the bureaucratic class and the political elite, and the people associated with them. [Next], most of [such] undertakings are in the service sector, mostly retails [such as] boutiques, cafes, brand retail, and suchlike. Moreover, [most of the] enterprises are largely of livelihood strategies, and not of the nature of innovative entrepreneurship and hence do not create [much gainful] employment opportunities . . . Lack of finance capital and basic infrastructure are major obstacles in establishing manufacturing enterprises. [To end with], there is an observed imitation (and lack of innovation) in going for entrepreneurial ventures, with most people flocking to do the same activity.

In addition to an infrastructural deficit – hard infrastructure (such as road connectivity, power availability and water supply) as well as soft infrastructure (such as human resource management skills, marketing skills, negotiation

skills and cash flow management skills), another major constraint for industrial development in Kohima as well as in the state is the problem of *levies*
from underground factions, which is arresting the economy of the state as a
whole. At least five major armed Naga political factions – fighting for a separate Naga nation state – collect or extort levies, which – in popular parlance –
is referred to as *unabated taxation*. Disquieting reports in the local media as
well as national media (see Karmakar, 2021 and The Eastern Mirror, 2021)
suggest of business establishments shifting to neighbouring states owing to
the adverse state of law and order, expressly, extortion over the barrel of a
gun. Such an adverse state of affairs is required to be urgently alleviated in
order to engender an enabling environment for private investment and consequently for the private sector to grow, which is necessary to gainfully employ
the demographic dividend of the state.

Notwithstanding all the above-stated concerns, however, in accordance
with the theory of urban agglomeration (as discussed earlier), Kohima along
with Dimapur, with the highest clustering of enterprises, are the biggest
agglomeration centres in Nagaland.

Trade and Commerce

In 2006, although about 18% of the workforce was engaged in trade and
commerce (GoN, 2006), the activities are – as noted earlier – restricted to
mostly retails. Commodities are mostly imported either from the neighbouring city of Dimapur in the state or from the cities of Guwahati and Jorhat in
the neighbouring state of Assam as well as from the city of Imphal in another
neighbouring state of Manipur, or from the city of Ludhiana in the faraway
state of Punjab, or from the metropolitan cities of Chennai, Delhi, Kolkata
and Mumbai in the country (GoN, 2006). All this underscores the salience
of Kohima as an important market for the producers of the region as well as
of the country as a whole. It also calls for an enhancement in connectivity to
further enhance the extant market connectivity, especially to find outlets for
the products of the city.

Tourism

Endowed with a distinctively scenic natural heritage as well as a uniquely
colourful cultural heritage, Kohima along with other districts of the state
attracts tourists from within and outside the country (see Table 4.3). The
climate in the state remains generally agreeable all through the year. Tourists
can therefore visit the state throughout the year, making the state one of the
favourite tourist destinations in NER. Concerning its natural heritage, the
picturesque mountainous sub-tropical rain forests with a plethora of flora
and fauna offers ample opportunities for adventure tourism (such as trek-
king, rock climbing and jungle camping). Concerning its cultural heritage,

Table 4.3 Number of tourist arrival

	Year		
Type	2000	2010	2019
Domestic	13,268	21,094	125,949
International	451	1132	5568
Total	13,791	22,226	131,517

Source: GoN (2013, 2022)

the central government identified the second largest number of tourism projects (51 projects) for Nagaland in the countrywide list (next only to Jammu and Kashmir with 88 projects) during its Eleventh Five Year Plan. All this reflects the tourism potential of the state.

Being relatively much more accessible (as suggested earlier) with a much more developed hospitality sector – possessing the second largest number of hotels and restaurants in the state (GoN, 2022) – as well as more developed tourist attraction spots as compared to the other districts of the state, Kohima receives a comparatively much larger number of tourists. Of the nine identified tourist spots in the district of Kohima (GoN, 2022), the notable attractions include Commonwealth Second World War Cemetery, Second World War Museum, Nagaland Sales Emporium, Khonoma Green Village (regarded as the first green village in the country), Dzukou Valley and Mount Japfu Peak. Since 2000, the now internationally acclaimed annual *Hornbill Festival*, celebrating the diverse cultural heritage of the tribes of Nagaland, is being staged at the Kisama Heritage Village in Kohima. In 2015, 2.34 lakh tourists flocked to Hornbill Festival (GoI, 2017).

As is evident from Table 4.3, although the number of domestic as well as international tourist arrival in the state suggests an increasing trend, the same is still much below the potential tourist inflow. GoN (2006) attributed such a below-potential inflow to the prevailing travel restrictions such as Restricted Area Permit (RAP) (as required by the Government of India) for foreign nationals as well as Inner Line Permit (ILP) (as required by the Government of Nagaland) for the nationals to enter Kohima and other parts of Nagaland. Also, infrastructural deficit and the perceived safety concern from the prevailing insurgency problem are other constraints for the growth of tourism.

Quality of Life

A city is ultimately about people, and the quality of urban life is what actually matters most. The quality of life in Kohima can be understood from the achievement of the district as a whole in the Human Development Index (HDI). HDI, originally published by United Nations Development Program

(UNDP), is a measurement of achievement in what are seen as fundamental dimensions of human development (namely, health, knowledge and standard of living) of a country. While an achievement of HDI value of above 0.800 (on a scale of 1) by a country makes it classified as a *very high* human development country, an achievement of a value between 0.700 and 0.799 makes a country classified as a *high* human development country, a value between 0.550 and 0.699 as a *medium* human development country, and a value below 0.550 as *low* human development country.

While the HDI score of the district increased from 0.64 in 2001 – ranking second among the districts of the state (GoN, 2004) – to a remarkably 0.82 in 2008 – a score comparable to developed nations (GoN, 2009), it declined to 0.66 in 2011 (GoN, 2017) – ranking second again among the districts of the state. Ignoring what appears to be an inconsistently anomalous score in 2008, the data suggests that the district of Kohima has not registered any notable progress in the constituting indices of HDI, and therefore remains as a *medium* human development district – a position consistent with the state's as well as the country's similar position.

In regard to Gender Development Index (GDI) – also originally published by UNDP and measures gender inequality in the achievement of the aforementioned constituting indices of HDI, although in terms of an absolute score, Kohima district registered a marginal increase from 0.54 in 2001 (GoN, 2004) to 0.59 in 2011 (GoN, 2017), it registered a drop in the ranking from second to third in the state. Again, the statistics suggests that the district has not registered any notable progress in the constituting indices of GDI, and therefore its women remain in the *medium* human development category.

In case of Human Poverty Index (HPI) – also published by UNDP and measures deprivation in longevity, knowledge and standard of living – a positive development is observed for the district of Kohima. HPI is measured on a scale of 100, with a higher value indicating a higher deprivation or poverty. The district's absolute score of HPI declined from 33.13 in 2001 (GoN, 2004) to 27.84 in 2011 (GoN, 2017), reflecting a reduction in deprivation – ranking third in the state in both the years. As is evident from the available index value, however, a long distance is still required to be traversed in order to reach the minimum goalpost of 0.

Six localities in Kohima have been notified as slums.[5] In 2001, about 26% of the population of the city resided in slums. Of the total BPL population, slum dwellers accounted for about 35%. The housing structure of such dwellers includes own-houses, rented-houses as well as *kutcha* structures. The quality of life of the slum residents is especially deplorable. Some of the notable problems such dwellers encounter include absence of even basic public amenities, vulnerability to landslide, choked open drains from waste dumping owing to grossly inadequate solid waste management, and the consequent frequent occurrences of diseases – reportedly a high incidence of water-borne diseases such as cholera and hepatitis (GoN, 2006).

Having surveyed the spatial as well as socio-economic profiles of Kohima, SWOT analysis of the city is presented in the following. Such an analysis is made after a theoretical review of SWOT analysis to ensure an informed employment of the same given its limitations.

SWOT Analysis: A Theoretical Review

SWOT analysis emerged in literature in the 1960s alongside the emergence of the concept of *strategy* as employed in business management. As such, it is generally used to evaluate the strengths, weaknesses, opportunities and threats involved either in a business strategy or in a business activity or a project or in an organization (Gürel and Tat, 2017). The employment of SWOT in urban planning is therefore uncommon. The same can be, however, gainfully employed for such a planning as demonstrated in the following. A SWOT analysis can be either a quantitative or a qualitative analysis. The nature of analysis employed in the following is of the latter descriptive method. An example of an application of the former quantitative SWOT analysis is a study conducted by Chang and Huang (2005), wherein strengths of container ports in East Asia are assessed and suggestions therefrom are made on an adoptable competing strategy for each.

Caveats in using SWOT study have been suggested in the literature.

If used simplistically, the SWOT framework is a 'naïve' tool which may lead to strategic errors. More detailed analysis using complementary frameworks can overcome SWOT's inherent shortfalls . . . SWOT should not be viewed as a static analytical tool with emphasis solely on its output.
(Pickton and Wright, 1998)

SWOT Analysis is an analysis technique that has a general perspective and presents general solutions. Details and specific issues are not the focus of SWOT Analysis . . . It is not possible to determine the priorities of the factors identified in SWOT Analysis.
(Gürel and Tat, 2017)

For a further detailed discussion on the advantages and disadvantages of SWOT analysis, a reading can made from Gürel and Tat (2017).

Given the nature of SWOT analysis, the assessment made in the following is of general and static nature, and therein also arise the limitations of the analysis made. Such an assessment can nonetheless serve as a stage for further specific and dynamic studies of the concerns identified in the said analysis – and therefore, such a complementary study is called for as a direction for future research. Of such concerns, that in relation to urban mobility in Kohima is accordingly taken up in the ensuing chapters of the book.

SWOT Analysis of Kohima

Supplementing the aforementioned detailed profiling of Kohima with additional information, Tables 4.4–4.7 highlight the notable (however, not in any way exhaustive) SWOT of Kohima respectively.

Table 4.4 Strengths of Kohima

Sectors	Strengths
Location and connectivity	i A strategic regional setting. ii A major transit route in NER.

Tourism potential	i Natural heritage:
	  a A picturesque landscape.
	ii Cultural heritage:
	  a Nagas are culturally known for hospitality.
	  b A cultural centre of all the Naga tribes.
	iii Historical heritage:
	  a The *Stalingrad of the East*, Battle of Kohima, was fought in Kohima, which is memorialized by the internationally acclaimed Commonwealth War Memorial sited within Kohima.
	  b A Second World War Museum is established in the outskirt of Kohima.
	  c A window to the past tribal community life of the Nagas, Kisama Heritage Village, is established in the outskirt of Kohima.
	iv A considerable English proficiency of the citizenry.

Trade and commerce	i A comparatively substantial (and expanding) labour market as well as market for goods and services. ii An export potential of traditional arts and crafts from Kohima.
Human capital	i A literate citizenry.[1] ii A potential for IT sector.[2]
Institutions	i A centre of administration, education and culture. ii A marked presence of a number of non-governmental organizations (NGOs). iii A characteristic presence of social capital.[3] iv A strong indication of an improved service delivery from Kohima Municipal Council (KMC).[4]
Safety perception	i An initiative undertaken for a safe city.[5]

Source: GoN (2006), GoN (2009), GoI (2017), author's observation

Notes
[1] A 91% literacy rate of the citizenry of Kohima.
[2] Nagaland ranks second in terms of State Web Portal in India GoI (2017). A software technology park is also established in Kohima.
[3] Of the 91% waste collection efficiency, 40% is achieved by community participation (GoI, 2017)
[4] KMC successfully undertook projects related to solid waste management, city abattoir, mapping of households for property taxation and so on. Furthermore, KMC's savings is growing at a rate of 10% annually (GoI, 2017).
[5] While eight high-mast-lights have been provided at major junctions for greater security, 860 street lights have been installed to reduce crime and theft in public spaces (GoI, 2017).

Table 4.5 Weaknesses of Kohima

Sectors	Weaknesses
Infrastructure	i A severe traffic congestion.
	ii An on-street parking owing to a grossly inadequate parking space.
	iii An inefficient traffic management.
	iv A grossly inadequate public transportation system, with an inefficient bus service system.
	v An inefficient provisioning of taxi stations as well as an inadequate amenity for the taxi service providers.
	vi A poorly maintained drainage system.[1]
	vii An acute shortage of water, expressly during dry winter season.
	viii A frequent power outage.
	ix An insufficient internet connectivity.[2]
	x All this adversely affects the productivity of economic activities in Kohima.
Governance	i Poor implementation of the notified building byelaws, development regulations, fire safety and other suchlike regulations; and thereby the observed unplanned, unregulated and haphazard growth of Kohima.
	ii A declining space for public utilities and public spaces (such as an absence of recreational space and so on).
	iii A negligible land ownership under Kohima's Administration (which can be converted into a recreational space[3] and so on).
Trade and commerce	i A poor infrastructure.
	ii A negligible industrial base.
	iii An absence of business capital in the community as well as from financial institutions.[4]
Heritage conservation	i. An inadequate awareness among the citizens about heritage conservation as well as the economic potential from the same.
Environment	i A vulnerability to landslide owing to the topography as well as climate of Kohima, which is further accentuated by a poor drainage system.
	ii A poor living condition.
	iii Water contamination with sewerage.
	iv Vehicular air pollution.
Slums	i Poverty.
	ii All the slums are located in environmentally sensitive or unsafe areas, and therefore vulnerable to landslide and suchlike vulnerabilities.
Institutional capacity	i An inadequate technical capacity among the officials of KMC.
	ii An inability to conduct municipal election.

Source: GoN (2006), GoN (2009), GoI (2017), author's observation

Notes

[1] In an environment sector voting, 59% of the citizens report about storm water mixing with wastewater (GoI, 2017).

[2] Under the Information and Communications Technology (ICT) sector priority voting, 78% and 22% of the citizens report receiving poor telecom service and inadequate internet connectivity respectively (GoI, 2017).technology park is also established in Kohima.

[3] A total of 45% of the citizens are of the opinion that an *individual land ownership right* is a major obstacle to an otherwise immediately required road expansion (GoI, 2017).

[4] Credit Deposit Ratio of Nagaland is reported at 0.27 as compared to the national average of 0.78. From the same, we can gauge that credit availability is grossly inadequate in the state as well as in the city (GoN, 2017).

Table 4.6 Opportunities of Kohima

Sectors	Opportunities
Location and connectivity	i A geographical proximity to Association of Southeast Asian Nations (ASEAN) countries. ii An envisioned Asian Highway-1 passes through Kohima. iii A potential for an international trade centre.
Urban renewal	i A prime land can be unlocked for development at the city centre by consolidating all government offices in the New Secretariat Complex as well as by relocating the existing military establishments outside the city core. ii A mitigation of traffic congestion as well as vehicular air pollution will cause an environmental enhancement, and thereby an improvement in citizen's health. iii An extensive geo-spatial mapping carried out by Kohima's Administration can be employed for spatial planning and suchlike.
Infrastructure	i A neglected pedestrian network of Kohima can be invigorated to create a *walkable* city. ii Constructing a bypass road can alleviate traffic congestion in Kohima by diverting outbound vehicles away from the main street of the city.
Tourism	i Kohima, being a hill station, is endowed with vantages along the streets with picturesque view of the valleys and distant hills. A value addition can be made to such vantages in order to transform the same into city landmarks for visitors. ii Promotion of *Brand Kohima* (by means of, implementing visual enhancement codes as well as regulatory compliance of the same and so on). iii The rich historical as well as cultural heritage, especially the unique festivals of Nagaland, can be further leveraged to promote tourism. iv A transit tourism can be promoted by leveraging the envisioned development of Asian Highway-1. v The rich local crafts have an opportunity to create a substantial business opportunity.

Source: GoN (2006), GoN (2009), GoI (2017), author's observation

Table 4.7 Threats of Kohima

Sectors	Threats
Infrastructure	i A further increase in pressure on infrastructure from the ongoing urbanization. ii A further deterioration in the state of water scarcity. iii A further deterioration in the state of solid waste management as well as sewage network. iv A further worsening of slum condition. v All this may exacerbate the *liveability*, *working efficiency*, *competitiveness* and *sustainability* of Kohima.

Sectors	Threats
Institutional and fiscal reforms	i An inadequate institutional capacity building contributing to non-implementation of institutional reforms.
	ii An inadequate fiscal reform for implementation of projects, expressly provision of infrastructure in a sustainable manner.
Disaster vulnerability	i Kohima is on Seismic Zone 5, and thereby extremely vulnerable to structural collapse owing to an earthquake.
	ii Landslide, especially during monsoon, is another threat to the haphazardly dense urban growth.
	iii An extremely limited open space makes it difficult to create evacuation areas (or shelter zones).

Source: GoN (2006), GoN (2009), GoI (2017), author's observation

Conclusion

What emerges from the above discussion is that Kohima exhibits agglomeration economies, and is in terms of almost all socio-economic indicators, comparatively better off than almost all the districts of the state. For myriad potentials, the economic salience of Kohima as an agglomeration centre for the state as well as the NER is immense. It is a centre of administration, education and healthcare, an important transit route for intra-state and inter-state logistics, and a market for jobs as well as goods and services offering a better remuneration to the farmers as well as other producers from within and outside the state. It possesses the potential to become an important international agglomeration centre in the foreseeable future, with the actualization of India's Act East Policy.

Towards realizing all the aforesaid potentials, and to achieve a sustainable growth of Kohima, the urban policy should leverage the strengths and opportunities of the city on the one hand, and mitigate the weaknesses and threats of the city on the other hand. Converting the many urban challenges into opportunities will contribute in actualizing the many expected gains from urbanization (as discussed in the previous Part II), and contribute towards making Kohima an agglomeration economies augmenting, a congestion diseconomies mitigating and a resource generating city.

A sustainably growing Kohima, by acting as an agglomeration centre, will promote an interaction among people from different tribes, regions, religions and cultures. Such an interface will arguably promote national integration at the national level, and facilitate in reducing the observed ongoing tribalism at the state level. A direct as well as an indirect economic cost arises from such a state of tribalism or from an absence of social cohesion. With proper planning and policy intervention, besides the agglomeration benefits, Kohima can therefore contribute to national integration.

Notes

1 The state of Nagaland was created only after the independence of India in 1963. Prior, under and after the British Raj, Nagaland was part of a district, Naga Hills District, under the then state of Assam.
2 *Mainland Indians* is a popular reference to Indians from outside NER by the people from the region, which has found a mention in academic reference as well.
3 Areas such as D Block, New Market, Midland, Upper Chandmari and PR. Hill.
4 Areas such as Super Market, Tibetan Market, Khedi Market and KMC Market.
5 Namely, North Block, Naga Bazaar, Kitsubozou/Chotu Basti, New Market, Dak lane and Porter lane.

References

Chang, Hsu-Hsi and Huang, Wen-Chih, *Application of a quantification SWOT analytical method* (Mathematical and Computer Modelling). Elsevier, Amsterdam, 2005.

Government of India, *Census of India*. Government of India, 2001. http://censusindia.gov.in/

Government of India, *Census of India*. Government of India, 2011. http://censusindia.gov.in/

Government of India, *Kohima smart city proposal*. Government of India, New Delhi, 2017.

Government of Nagaland, *City development plan*. Government of Nagaland, 2006. www.nagaland.gov.in/

Government of Nagaland, *District human development report – Kohima*. Government of Nagaland, 2009. www.in.undp.org/

Government of Nagaland, *Gender statistics Nagaland: 2022*. N V Press, Kohima, 2022.

Government of Nagaland, *Nagaland state human development report*. Government of Nagaland, 2004. www.in.undp.org/

Government of Nagaland, *Nagaland state human development report*. Government of Nagaland, 2017. www.nagaland.gov.in/

Government of Nagaland, *Statistical handbook of Nagaland*. N V Press, Kohima, 2013.

Government of Nagaland, *Statistical handbook of Nagaland*. N V Press, Kohima, 2022.

Gürel, Emet and Tat Merba, *SWOT analysis: a theoretical review*. The Journal of International Social Research, 10(51), 2017. www.sosyalarastirmalar.com.

Ivan Su, Shong-Iee, Fisher Ke, Jian-Yu and Lim, Paul, *The development of transportation and logistics in Asia: an overview*. Transportation Journal, 50(1), 124–136, 2011.

Karmarkar, Rahul, Taxation by armed groups forcing businesses out: Nagaland trade body. *The Hindu*, 2021. https://www.thehindu.com/news/national/other-states/taxation-by-armed-groups-forcing-businesses-out-nagaland-trade-body/article34066697.ece

Pickton, David W and Wright, Sheila, *What's SWOT in strategic analysis?* Strategic Change, 7, 101–109, 1998.

The Eastern Mirror, Unabated taxation forcing business centres out of Nagaland, says DCCI. *The Eastern Mirror*, 2021. https://easternmirrornagaland.com/unabated-taxation-forcing-business-centres-out-of-nagaland-dcci/

Walling, Limakumba S and Humtsoe, Tumbenthung Y, *Political economy of development in the Indian state of Nagaland: issues and challenges*. Indian Journal of Human Development. https://doi.org/10.1177/09737030211062094 journals.sagepub.com/home/jhd, 2021

5 Theoretical Lessons for Sustainable Urban Mobility

Introduction

The ongoing urbanization is generating an upsurge in demand for basic urban services. Of such, urban mobility represents a critical wheel that either makes a city going and running or slows down and holds back a city, otherwise supposed to be a green engine of growth. The critical salience of urban mobility in the development of an urban space, and thereby the quality of life in such a space, is already explicated in an earlier chapter. An efficient green urban mobility service plying on an adequately connected network of transport infrastructure contributes to the *liveability, working efficiency, competitiveness* and *sustainability* of an urban agglomeration, which spills over to the entire economy contributing to sustainable economic development.

Against such a backdrop, the existing poor state of urban transport in Kohima (as presented in the following) is an immediate concern. Owing primarily to an absence of planning as well as inertia of policy intervention, the existing urban mobility system in Kohima is grossly in short supply as compared to the growing demand for commuting. In order to ensure that the currently underperforming green engine of growth, Kohima, performs optimally, it is urgently imperative to address the extant urban mobility concerns and challenges.

A glaring concern of urban mobility that stands out is the almost immobile traffic congestion on Kohima's main street – primarily for supply side inadequacies (as argued in the present chapter). The same is holding the city at a standstill, giving rise to substantial economic loss, environmental pollution as well as adverse health bearing. It appears that strategic lessons from Economics have not been incorporated in the urban mobility planning and provision – in the main an anticipatory planning of an integrated land use–transportation policy and suchlike, and therefore the chapter argues for such.

A model based on an *extended speed function* as well as an *extended cost function* – as distinct from the standard speed and cost functions (as explained in the following) – and a traffic demand curve is developed to show that in a scenario of congestion with Kohima-like characteristics, supply side

DOI: 10.4324/9781032711799-8

intervention may be an *initial* efficient as well as an equitable action. In a way, it answers the question of *which should precede which, supply side or demand side interventions, given the idiosyncrasies of a given context.* Also intended in the current chapter is to demonstrate how an efficient as well as an effective policy prescription can be drawn from a theoretical model.

History of Connectivity

A history of modern transport infrastructure in the context of Kohima as well as that of Nagaland, which began with the dawn of colonial history in Naga Hills, is a history of road. What existed prior were just 'circuitous, steep, and little more than animal tracks, jagged pathways, winding tracks, impracticable roads' (Dzuvichu, 2013) connecting villages, and villages to fields as well as to the foothill markets in the Assam plain. 'In laying out colonial roads, [however,] the existing pathway was usually preferred [and] engineering skills of the hill people' were also employed for the same (Dzuvichu, 2013).

Such a road was, however, not constructed to facilitate development as is generally done today. The same was meant to facilitate British conquest and the subsequent *controlling* of the natives to support the administration in the hills. 'To bring the Nagas and other hill tribes under control, what was required, declared Lieutenant John Butler, the Political Agent of Naga Hills, in May 1873, was to open out their country by good bridle paths' (Dzuvichu, 2013). A road construction therefore became a strategic colonial policy, and 'a flurry of activities involving the construction of a network of bridle paths thus ensued in the 1870s.' Such 'road-building projects were largely organized with military priorities in mind and their architects were military men like Colonel Johnstone' (Dzuvichu, 2013). Even at the beginning of the 20th century, however, colonial roads were still largely either 'bridle paths' or at the most 'all weather cart roads.' In 1903–1904, the total length of road in the Naga Hills was 73 miles of cart road and 470 miles of bridle paths (Dzuvichu, 2013).

Such a road extension in the state began roughly from west to east. Expressly, from Samaguting, where the British entering from Assam in the west established its first administrative headquarter in 1866, and then, with the seriatim subjugation over the different Naga tribes – Angamis, Rengmas, Lothas, Aos and then Sumis respectively – a road made inroad to the traditional territories of the tribes – Kohima, Wokha, Mokukchung and Zunheboto successively. Of note from such a nature of road extension is that Kohima received a head start in colonial road provisioning.

The Second World War came, and road construction picked up as part of war preparation. A biography of a grandmother, *Mari*, by a well-known novelist from Nagaland, Kire (2010), captured the frantic road construction against a looming war, wherein the native subjects were even contracted by the colonial masters for construction in an attempt to accelerate road building. After the War, however, there was practically no further enhancement until the year 1957 when Naga Hills Tuensang Area (NHTA) was formed as a separate administrative unit under the province of Assam. Nonetheless, not much expansion of road capacity was registered (Nagaland Board of School Education, 2015).

A considerable expansion was to come only after the statehood of Nagaland in 1963. From just 837 km at the time of statehood (GoN, 2004), the total road length increased to 12,033 km in 2012–2013 (GoN, 2014). Thereafter, many more motor-able roads sprang up connecting almost all villages with the administrative headquarters. By 2002–2003, about 79% of villages were connected by roads (GoN, 2004). The road network, however, still remains unsatisfactory in quantity as well as in quality in both Kohima and the rest of the state (Humtsoe, 2020), as shall be explicated later in the case of the former.

Mitigating Traffic Congestion: Literature Review

Humtsoe (2022) summarized traffic congestion mitigation as follows:

> Traffic congestion can be mitigated either solely through Supply Side Management (SSM) or solely through Demand Side Management (DSM), or through a combination of [both]. While SSM usually takes the form of (but not exclusively of) enhancing road capacity, DSM usually takes the form of pricing/cost policies and to a lesser extent through command and control policies.

On the one hand, a recurring supply side intervention is fiscally as well as environmentally unsustainable, and after a certain threshold becomes even counter-productive – a case of Downs-Thomson paradox. The stated well documented empirical paradox suggests that an enhancement in road capacity can contrarily worsen a traffic congestion by means of either making the mode of public transport more inconvenient or making the mode of personalized transport more convenient (and thereby shifting commuters away from the former to the latter). Such a paradox is also observed in Indian cities wherein, 'efforts by city authorities to augment roads and construct flyovers are nullified by the increase in ownership of personalised vehicles, induced traffic volume and return of congestion' (Mishra, 2019).

On the other hand, the effectiveness of pricing policy (a demand side intervention) is crucially contingent on the degree of price elasticity[1] (the higher the degree, the more the effectiveness, and vice versa), which declines over time – as is evident from literature. Concerning an evidence of short-run price elasticity, it is reported that the short-run price elasticity of gasoline demand in the US decreased from −0.034 to −0.077 between 2001 and 2006, as against from −0.21 to −0.34 between 1975 and 1980 (Hughes et al., 2008). Concerning an evidence of long-run price elasticity, it is reported that the long-run price elasticity of fuel demand in the US also decreased in scale over time between 1966 and 2001 (Small and Dender, 2007).

A scant literature exists that answers the question posed in the present study: given the unique challenges, opportunities as well as priorities of a given context, whether supply side or demand side interventions should precede? It is therefore envisaged to provide preliminary as well as original evidence towards addressing that gap by drawing lessons from a theoretical model constructed in the following.

Extended Speed Function and Extended Cost Function

Traffic congestion is a condition on a road network characterized by an exceedingly slow traffic speed measured in relation to a given optimal speed (not necessarily a completely congestion-free speed), creating an increased vehicular queuing as well as a longer trip time. From literature, it emerges that although common congestion measurement metrics are 'speed, travel time, [travel time] delay and volume and level of service' (Rao and Rao, 2012), almost all the countries define congestion in terms of a reduced vehicular speed on a particular stretch, and accordingly devise a policy intervention. The yardstick of a congestion threshold speed, however, varies inter-countries as well as intra-country. In accordance with the prevalent practice, a speed metric of congestion is employed in the current theoretical frame as well.

The textbook conceptualization of a traffic congestion in a graphical model is the so-called *speed function* (adapted from Humtsoe, 2020; see also Button, 2010). In such a speed function, traffic speed (S) is taken as a function of the number of vehicles per lane hour (T). Algebraically, speed function (S) can be written as follows:

$$S = S(T)$$
$$dS \, / \, dT \leq 0,$$

wherein, as T increases, S may or may not decrease. If traffic speed falls, it means a *marginal vehicle* (or simply, an additional car) causes congestion. Otherwise, no congestion is created.

By explicitly introducing a new variable denoting *traffic congestion easing supply side interventions* in the function, and redefining the above independent variable T as number of commuters per capacity hour (and not as the number of vehicles per lane hour), an *extended speed function* is proposed, bearing in mind the idiosyncrasies characterizing traffic congestion in Kohima. By means of the said addition in the standard model, congestion is made a function not only of lane and time, but also of other supply side transport infrastructure and services (denoted by capacity, *C*) explicitly in the function itself. Algebraically, the extended speed function (S′) can be written as follows:

$$S' = S(T, C).$$
$$S = C / T,$$

wherein, with constant C numerator, S falls if T rises; and with constant T, S rises if C increases, or S falls if C decreases. In other words, with the numerator (C) remaining unchanged, the traffic speed (S) decreases/increases with the increase/decrease in the denominator (T).

As C increases, ceteris paribus, the *congestion threshold* – after which traffic speed falls – increases. When a capacity is expanded, either the same or a greater number of commuters – not necessarily more number of vehicles (which is otherwise the case with a road capacity extension) – can travel at the same time without causing congestion externalities on an otherwise previously congested motorway. Such a case is graphically explained in Figure 5.1.

In the upper panel of Figure 5.1, while the y-axis measures traffic speed (S), the x-axis measures the number of commuters per *capacity* per hour (T). At the initial capacity represented by C in the extended speed function, S′ = S(T, C), the congestion threshold is Tp number of commuters per hour. After the capacity is enhanced to C*, the congestion threshold increases to

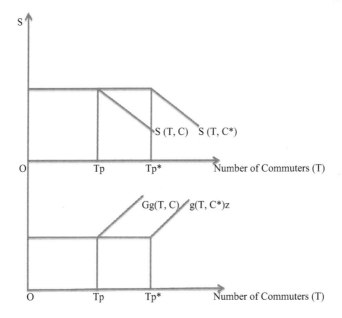

Figure 5.1 Extended speed function and extended congestion cost function.

Tp*. In perspective, TpTp* greater number of commuters can be accommodated without producing congestion externalities.

A reference to the general set of transportation costs is apposite before a further discussion on the particular subset of the same, specifically, the cost of traffic congestion. Such a set of costs, to begin with, can be further categorized into monetary cost and non-monetary cost. While the former includes such nature of costs that are directly quantifiable in monetary terms (such as fares, fuel cost and vehicle operating cost), the latter includes such nature of costs that are not directly quantifiable in monetary terms (such as trip time, reliability and comfort level of travel). An understanding of the said categorization is necessary to clearly comprehend the concept of congestion cost function (as shall be seen in the following).

The mirror image of the extended speed function, $S' = S(T, C)$, is the *extended congestion cost function*, $g' = g(T, C)$ (as opposed to the standard congestion cost function), represented in the lower panel of Figure 5.1. In perspective, congestion cost is taken as a function of traffic speed (specifically, traffic congestion). Such a derivation of a cost function from a speed function can be explained from the positive relationship obtainable between commuting cost and congestion (say, when traffic congestion increases, commuting cost – monetary as well as non-monetary – increases, and vice versa). In perspective, when traffic congestion increases, not only monetary commuting cost (say, fuel cost) rises (say, owing to burning more gasoline driving in lower gears), but also non-monetary commuting cost (say, trip time) increases. The commuting cost of increased trip time and increased fuel consumption 'are estimated to amount to hundreds of dollars per capita per year in the US and comparable . . . [estimates] reported for Europe' (Lindsey and Verhoef, 2000).

In the lower panel of Figure 5.1, while the y-axis measures congestion cost (g), the x-axis measures the number of commuters per *capacity* per hour (T). In cases of pre-capacity expansion as well as post-capacity expansion, the commuting cost owing to congestion increases after crossing the congestion thresholds, Tp and Tp*, respectively. A congestion cost curve, such as $g(T, C)$, after the congestion threshold, such as Tp, need not necessarily be a linear curve (as depicted in Figure 5.1), and the shape can vary over time as well. An extreme possibility of such a non-linear curve is a case of a hyper-congestion where the curve may even bend backwards (see Lindsey and Verhoef, 2000). Similarly, in a case where capacity – as defined earlier – decreases, a backward bending curve may also arise, for congestion can occur in a previously congestion-free quantum of T (say, before Tp).

Using the concepts elucidated in the present section, a context informed model of congestion mitigation is developed in regard to the almost immobile urban mobility in Kohima (as explicated in the succeeding section). In essence, traffic congestion is a condition of mismatch between supply (capacity) and demand, requiring supply side interventions as well as demand side interventions for the mitigation of the same. The relative efficiency as well as comparative practicality between supply side approach and demand side approach, or the question of precedence between such approaches, in the context of Kohima, is assessed in terms of the said model. The state of urban mobility in Kohima, however, is initially presented.

State of Urban Mobility

As alluded to earlier, the major urban mobility concerns confronting the city of Kohima are traffic congestion and vehicular air pollution.

Traffic Congestion

As mentioned earlier, traffic congestion is mostly expressed in terms of an experiential traffic speed profile in relation to an optimal traffic speed. In 2006, the overall traffic speed of Kohima varied between 14 and 25 km/h, with an even lower traffic speed in downtown at about 5 km/h (GoN, 2006), which is either comparable to or even lower than the speed recorded in other metropolitan Indian cities. For comparison, the average journey speed in Delhi was around 16 km/h in 2007, and it was only slightly higher in Mumbai – which recorded a speed of 5 km/h only during peak hour (Alam and Ahmed, 2013). Similarly, the average journey speed was recorded to be below 20 km/h in other metropolises of Hyderabad, Chennai and Bangalore (Alam and Ahmed, 2013). It therefore indicates that smaller cities of the extent of Kohima are confronting diseconomies of traffic congestion rather prematurely.

Given the inadequate PTS in Kohima as well as the growing aspiration of people to own a car consequent to a rising income, private cars are mushrooming on the more or less static road capacity, further accentuating the traffic congestion. Accordingly, as compared to the traffic speed registered in 2006 (as stated earlier), 'the speed profile indeed dropped to 6 km/h . . . a fall of 13 km/h in about a decade's time' (Humtsoe, 2022). Such a process is augmented by a thriving used-car market in the state, with more affordable used cars coming in from as far as Delhi. The same creates an adverse implication for vehicular air pollution for vehicular emission generally increases with an age of a vehicle. Indicatively, the registered motor vehicles in Nagaland rose by 64% between 2002 and 2012 (North Eastern Council, 2015).

Nagaland Vision 2030 document (GoN, 2016) terms the prevailing traffic situation in Kohima as 'clogged traffic.' Smart City Proposal of Kohima (GoI, 2017) reported that '47 percent of the [city's] citizens considered poor road condition as the major problem in transportation sector priority voting, followed by traffic congestion attaining 32 percent.'

Vehicular Air Pollution

From health as well as ecological standpoint, another immediate concern is the observed rising air pollution in Kohima. It is clear from Table 5.1 that in

Table 5.1 Annual average concentration of particulate matter

Years	Station			
	Opposite NST Office		Opposite War Cemetery	
	RSPM	*SPM*	*RSPM*	*SPM*
2011	62	106	92	195
2012	63	107	100	217
2013	66	128	104	238
2014	71	142	113	251

Source: Nagaland Pollution Control Board (2016)

the recent years, the particulate matter contaminants in the city are registering an increasing trend. Moreover, the level of respirable suspended particulate matter (RSPM) has exceeded the prescribed National Ambient Air Quality Standard (NAAQS) value of 60 $\mu g/m^3$. Similarly, even in the case of suspended particulate matter (SPM), the level has exceeded the prescribed annual standard of 140 $\mu g/m^3$. It is a cause of much worry for RSPM as well as SPM are causative agents of morbidity as well as mortality. In accordance with the causality between air pollution and respiratory diseases, a senior pulmonologist at the largest hospital in Kohima (as well as in the state) expectedly reported a noticeably increasing pattern in such ailments among patients from urban areas in recent years. Air pollution therefore engenders an economic cost (not only in terms of treatment cost for respiratory ailments but also in terms of loss of potential earning during the course of treatment).

Nagaland Pollution Control Board (NPCB) (2016) attributes such an increasing trend to various factors such as inferior road condition, increasing vehicular movements and burning of waste. Data for the whole year of 2014 (available on NPCB website) indicates that air pollution becomes more severe during winter. Winter months being dry, the streets become dustier. An absence of street-sweeping as well as a clogged drainage along the street of the city accentuate the problem (Humtsoe, 2020). Another aspect of an adverse health bearing arising especially from a kutcha road (dusty when sunny and muddy when raining) is that it not only directly discourages walking – which is a health improving non-motorized mode of commuting – but also indirectly encourages motorized mode of commuting – which exacerbates vehicular pollution and thereby adverse health effect as well. Accordingly, a negligible road paving is being undertaken under the National Clean Air Programme (NCAP) in the city. Such an undertaking should be adequately as well as urgently extended in order to alleviate the deteriorating air pollution in the city. On the whole, it emerges from the ongoing discussion on the causal aspects of air pollution in Kohima that the said pollution emanates primarily from its urban transport sector. It is therefore urgently imperative to address the concerns and challenges of urban mobility to also address the concerns related to ecology as well as health arising from the same.

As mentioned earlier, the aforesaid traffic congestion in Kohima and the consequent growing environmental as well as health concerns can be construed as arising from a mismatch between supply of transport and demand for transport, and the same is discussed in the following.

Demand for Transport

A demand for transport is basically a derived demand created by a need for travel between a trip origin and a trip destination, which crucially depends on the nature of demography (say, the larger the population, the larger the demand for travel) as well as the state of an economy (say, the richer the economy, the larger the demand for travel – such as for domestic tourism). Another significant determining factor is the state of an urban planning (say, the better the planning, the smaller the demand for travel). Such significant factors contributing to the demand for transport in Kohima are discussed under the following sub-sections.

Strategic Central Location

Kohima, as mentioned in the preceding Chapter 4, is strategically located and acts as a transit route for intra-state as well as inter-state logistics. It shares boundaries with two states of the country as well as five districts of the state. Altogether, three National Highways originate from or traverse through or terminate in the city.

Kohima's road network is 'overburdened by the heavy goods vehicles moving through the national highways passing through the city. The same causes congestion in the city's core' (GoN, 2006). On an average, City Development Plan of Kohima (GoN, 2006) reported that about 4700 vehicles enter and exit Kohima in 12-hour duration (although an updated data is unavailable, such a number of vehicles must have certainly increased as of today). Of the total vehicles, cars (over 70%) and goods vehicles (about 15%) are the predominant modes constituting 85% of total traffic. Such vehicles entering and exiting the city – from and to neighbouring villages, towns and states – significantly contribute to the total traffic volume of the city. The modes of vehicle as well as selected location wise traffic volume (where check-posts existed, and thereby facilitated counting of vehicles in passage) are detailed in Table 5.2. Again, although an updated statistics on the same is unavailable, such a stated pattern of modes will be more or less consistent even at present. The total number of vehicles must have, however, certainly increased – especially considering the observed increasing volume of trade as well as the number of vehicles in the state, region and across the country. It is also reflected in the snowballing state of congestion observed across the years.

Table 5.2 Mode and traffic volume (number of vehicles)

Mode	Location					
	Bypass Check Post	Merema Check Post (NH-61)	Phezema Check Post (NH-39)	Border Security Force (BSF) Camp Check Post	Secretariat Road	Overall
Two-wheeler	50	33	70	21	168	342 (5%)
Cars	1529	459	853	522	1395	4758 (74%)
Buses	113	17	87	47	99	363 (6%)
Goods vehicles	472	78	254	85	81	970 (15%)
Total	2164 (34%)	587 (9%)	1264 (20%)	675 (10%)	1743 (27%)	6433 (100%)

Source: GoN (2006)

As reported earlier, the strategic central location of Kohima contributes to its volume of traffic, creating an enormous pressure on the existing grossly inadequate two-lane road capacity. In the city's urban mobility planning, therefore, a regulation of regional traffic (including segregation of regional traffic from urban traffic by means of a bypass road) is an important aspect.

Centre of Administration, Education, Healthcare and Tourism

Being the capital of the state, Kohima is the central administrative, educational, healthcare, commercial as well as cultural centre of Nagaland. As an administrative hub, while *administrative land use* accounted for the highest land use in the city (as mentioned in the previous chapter 4), a majority of the workforce in the city is similarly engaged in the government sector (again, as reported in the preceding chapter 4). As an education hub, Kohima accommodates the highest and the second highest number of government colleges and private colleges in the state respectively. As a healthcare hub, Kohima again accommodates the highest number of doctors as well as medical specialists in the state (GoN, 2022). Accordingly, people from within the state and outside agglomerate in the city for work, education and healthcare. Such an agglomeration occasions a growing trade and commerce (detailed later), which further augments the said agglomeration. All this thereby creates inter alia a demand for conveyance. Furthermore, being comparatively more accessible as well as having a more developed hospitality sector as compared to the other districts (as discussed in the preceding chapter 4), Kohima draws a relatively greater number of tourists. Of note, during the annual Hornbill Festival (when, as highlighted in the preceding chapter 4, the cultural heritage of all the tribes of the state is at full display, further adding to the stature of Kohima as the cultural capital of the state), local, domestic as well as international tourists flock to the city. A standstill traffic flow is common during the time of the said festival.

Population Growth

Reflecting the pull factors (or centripetal forces) of Kohima (some of which are briefed in the preceding sub-section in terms of the city being a centre of administration, education, healthcare and tourism), while the decadal growth rate of the state was negative (−0.48%) in 2011, it was over 28% for Kohima (GoI, 2011). The population of the city as well as its share in the state's overall population is expectedly projected to increase as shown in Table 5.3. The demand for urban mobility is accordingly bound to rise. It calls for an anticipatory urban mobility planning as well as investment incorporating the said population projection.

Table 5.3 Population projection

Year	Population	Compound Annual Growth Rate	Percentage of State's Population
2021	176,166	1.7	6.96
2031	208,512	1.7	7.42
2041	246,797	1.7	7.95

Source: GoN (2006)

Nature of Urbanization

As stated in the Nagaland Vision 2030 document (GoN, 2016), 'the urbanization pattern [in the state] is somewhat skewed as the urban growth is concentrated in few key towns such as Dimapur and Kohima.' Accordingly (as mentioned in the previous chapter 4), the difference in the rate of urbanization between that of Kohima district and that of the state as a whole doubled – from 8% in 2001 to about 16% in 2011 (GoI, 2011). Against the backdrop of a grossly inadequate investment in urban mobility, such a trend – reflecting immigration into the city – exerts an enormous pressure on the intra-city mobility system.

Concerning migrants from within the state, MIG and HIG, as discussed in the preceding chapter 4, show the maximum tendency of coming into the city. In perspective, groups possessing a means to access congestion augmenting personalized modes of mobility are coming into the city. Concerning migrants from outside the state, as discussed again in the previous chapter 4, MPG shows the maximum tendency of coming into the city. In perspective again, a group requiring an adequate provision of PTS is coming into the city. Against the said backdrop, the inadequacy of PTS in quantity (especially to cater to the MPG) as well as in quality (especially to induce the MIG and HIG to shift away from congestion accentuating personalized modes to congestion easing PTS) is required to be immediately addressed.

Market

Given the size and nature of the city's demography, with relatively more people and comparatively more better-off people residing in the city than in other districts of the state, the market size of Kohima is not only wider but also offers a better remuneration. Goods vehicles accounting for 15% of the total number of vehicles entering and exiting the city (GoN, 2006) suggests the salience of the city in terms of a market. Traders in local merchandise from across the state and beyond (from Manipur in the main) come to the city to trade. Similarly, traders in manufactured merchandise agglomerate in the city from across the country and beyond (mainly from Tibet and Nepal) to trade.

Villagers from across the state and beyond (from Burma in the main) come to the city to work primarily as informal domestic workers, but also in the other sub-sectors of the informal service sector. It is also common for people from across the state to come to the city for shopping, especially during festive seasons. The pull factor of market therefore causes agglomeration of traders, shoppers as well as job seekers. As stated in the foregoing chapter 4, the number of employed people (in public sector as well as private sector) is accordingly highest in the district of Kohima. All this not only enhances the demand for intra-city conveyance but also augments the intra-city traffic volume.

Occupational Structure

As reported in the preceding chapter 4, while the workforce participation rate in Kohima shows an upward movement, the proportion of the overall marginal workforce exhibits a fluctuating movement. Again, as suggested in the previous chapter 4, the occupational profile of Kohima suggests a substantial presence of workers and traders in the informal economy, unemployed workforce and students. Given the absence of an integrated agglomeration-mobility planning (as alluded to before, and as discussed in the following), while the increasing trend of workforce suggests an increasing derived demand for conveyance, the acute scarcity of employment prospect in the formal economy suggests that the unemployed and the employed in the informal sector have to travel longer distance in search of work and commute longer distance for work respectively.

Land-Use Pattern

In addition to a substantial composition of informal workers (as stated earlier), the occupational profile of Kohima, as reported in the preceding chapter 4, shows that a majority of the workforce is engaged in the government sector (GoN, 2006). Given the absence of an urban planning (specifically, an integrated land use–transport strategy), such a nature of composition further raises the demand for conveyance. In perspective, given that offices are generally constructed sans residential quarters in proximity, more government employees translate into more conveyance for work purpose. Of note, the New Capital Complex, within which are sited the government secretariat as well as most of the departmental directorates, is developed at the northern end of the city without adequate quarters. Office personnel therefore commute for work from the central part as well as from the southern end of the city. In order to eliminate such a potentially eliminable growth in the demand for travel, an integrated land use and transport planning is imperative.

Supply of Transport

Having discussed the demand side for mobility in Kohima, the supply side of transport is discussed in the following.

Road System

The topography of Kohima is such that a steep slope and a narrow valley often separate each residential area from the next creating a difficulty of technical nature for road provision. Such a terrain governs the shape of the road network development, which generally traverses along the elongated city. A national highway connects Kohima with the westernmost district of the state, Dimapur, where the currently sole airport as well as the main operational railway station of the state are located, and the same highway further connects the western part of Kohima with the southern part, which then, passing through semi-urban and rural areas, connects the city with the neighbouring state of Manipur in the south. While another national highway connects the northern part of Kohima with the northern districts of the state (Wokha and Mokukchung), a different highway connects the eastern part of the city with the district of Phek in the east. In addition to such national highways, a network of generally narrow streets connects the neighbourhoods of the city.

The major road network of Kohima increased from a grossly inadequate 15 km in 2006 (GoN, 2006) to a still inadequate 87 km in 2015 (GoI, 2017); of which, about 55% of the road network was of a single lane configuration in 2006 (a carriageway of 6 m or less) (GoN, 2006). Coupled with the growing number of vehicles (as suggested earlier), since neither any extension of the extant road network nor any widening of the extant carriageway of the road have been made, traffic congestion is going from bad to worse. Smart City Proposal of Kohima (GoI, 2017) reported that '47 % of the citizens considered poor road condition as the major problem in transportation sector priority voting, followed by traffic congestion attaining 32 % of citizen's priority.' Similarly, more than 78% of the citizens expressed the need for additional roads (GoN, 2009).

In addition to an inadequacy of road capacity in terms of quantity, the same is also insufficient in terms of quality. Most of the road intersections are either T or X shaped, with an inefficient geometric engineering (GoN, 2006). Such an inefficient road geometry not only slows down the traffic speed (as drivers have to decelerate to navigate) but also increases the probability of road accident. Such an accident – in addition to causing mortality, morbidity and other such economic as well as social costs – further slows down traffic speed, thereby snowballing the economic loss by adversely affecting logistics in transit. 'The major cause of accidents is lack of proper road geometry and ill-designed intersections with inadequate sight distance. Trucks, taxis, and LCVs [Light Commercial Vehicles] are reportedly involved in 75 percent of the accidents' (GoN, 2006).

Given the central location of Kohima, and the consequent high volume of intra-state as well as inter-state vehicles in transit, it is immediately imperative to enhance the currently inadequate bypasses. Such an immediate salience of the same is also established from the following observation:

> The recently constructed inter-urban road, referred to as 'short-cut' by the users of the road, begins from the outskirt of Kohima, and cuts the travel time significantly for those traveling from Tuensang, Mokukchung, Wokha and other areas to the commercial hub, Dimapur. However, the road [is not] in use for over a year [owing] to lack of maintenance. Vehicles [therefore] take the . . . longer road (implying longer travel time) [that passes through the] Kohima city, accentuating traffic congestion and air pollution of the city.
>
> (Humtsoe, 2020)

Parking

Reflecting (as well as owing to) the inadequate accessibility as well as connectivity within Kohima, commercial establishments are concentrated alongside the central street of the elongated city. Alongside the same commercial areas, the extant demand for parking space considerably exceeds the grossly inadequate supply of such a space. On the side of supply, the parking capacity increased from only 1 in 2012 to still only 9 in 2015 (GoI, 2017). In addition to the inadequate bypasses as mentioned earlier, given the absence of a designated bus as well as a truck terminal, the entry of such heavy vehicles into Kohima accentuates the congestion within the city (GoN, 2006). On the side of demand, even in 2006, the peak parking demand by mode varies between 80 Equivalent Car Space[2] (ECS) and 130 ECS. Of which, the maximum demand came from cars (GoN, 2006), suggesting a policy implication of shifting away from congestion accentuating cars towards congestion easing PTS. Owing to the stated mismatch between supply and demand, users of vehicle navigate an extra distance (worsening congestion in doing so) spending an extra time in order to find a space to park. Such an extra distance driven as well as an extra time spent by modes of vehicles in 2006 are given in Table 5.4. Given the growing demand against a stagnant supply, the statistics concerning the same must have certainly increased as of present.

Table 5.4 Extra distance and extra time for parking

Mode	Extra Travel Distance (m)	Extra Travel Time (min)
Cars	50	3
Taxi	50	3
Two-wheeler	40	3

Source: GoN (2006)

In certain commercial as well as institutional areas (such as schools, colleges and offices), a limited parking space is available, however, since 'taxi stands are not properly planned' (GoI, 2017) and given that the said availability is considerably limited, most of such a space is occupied by taxis. As a result of the same, an unauthorized on-street parking by shoppers encroaches on the already narrow carriageway, endangering the jostling pedestrians as well as accentuating congestion furthermore. Above all, an authorized on-street parking occupies 6 m and more of the carriageway. If relieved by means of an off-street parking, it is estimated that the present traffic speed of about 17–20 km/h might increase to as much as 25–35 km/h (GoI, 2017). In consideration of all this, the much-delayed completion of the ongoing construction of off-street multi-storey parking spaces in Kohima ought to be immediately operationalized.

Above all, another reason for an on-street parking is an absence of parking space either within a residential building or within a commercial building alongside the streets of Kohima. Occupants of such buildings therefore engage in on-street parking. A policy implication that emerges from such a state is the necessity of an integrated building-transport urban policy. A provision of parking spaces should be mandated in building regulations to eliminate on-street parking arising from the absence of the same.

Footpaths

A quantitatively as well as qualitatively adequate provision of footpaths as well as footbridges encourages walking, a non-motorized mode of mobility. Such non-motorized modes

> are the best transportation means on any criteria. It is friendly to the environment and climate . . . various socioeconomic and sustainability potential . . . such as control over greenhouse gas emissions, control over congestion, control over environmental pollution, and avoidance of fossil fuel use for shorter trips . . . flexibility in use and the affordability . . . improved access to work at affordable pricing, employment generation potential.
>
> (Yedla, 2015)

Against the aforesaid salience of such a mode, the extant state of footpaths as well as footbridges in Kohima is a concern.

Although a footpath exists on all the major stretches of the central street of the city, a guardrail exists in some stretches only (GoN, 2006). Since the insufficiently narrow footpath is constructed alongside an insufficiently narrow street, such an absence adversely affects the safety of the jostling pedestrians from the plying vehicles. The inadequately maintained drainage system along the footpath further worsens the safety of the pedestrians. From such a state of drains, an overflow of rainwater combined with slush, untreated sewage as well as other wastes adversely affects the walkability quotient of the city (GoI, 2017). Of note concerning the walkability quotient is the climate of Kohima (with a heavy precipitation for the greater part of the year), which necessitates not only an adequately maintained drainage system but also a currently absent roof over a footpath. Above all, the inadequate provision of pedestrian footbridges slows down traffic speed as vehicles have to either stop or decelerate to make the pedestrians cross over.

Transport Service Providers

While private cars, private bus service providers, public bus service providers (operated by Kohima Municipal Council) and private taxis (owned by private individuals – generally Kohima residents – and are operated either by the owners themselves or by employed drivers) – with no presence of corporate taxi aggregators – constitute the passenger carrier vehicles, only privately operated vehicles constitute the goods carrier vehicles. In 2015, while the registered number of private taxis and that of private buses were 713 and 109 respectively, the number of public buses was only 25 (GoI, 2017). The provision of transportation services is therefore mostly from the private sector (as shall be seen in the following chapter as well).

The singular mode of PTS (expressly, bus service) 'is [also] unstructured and inefficient, adding to the . . . [traffic] congestion by their long stoppages to collect passengers. These buses further block the narrow roads at the bus stops' (GoI, 2017). Moreover, such a PTS is available only along the singular stretch of the main street, leaving most areas of the city un-served. Against such a background of a grossly inadequate PTS, a congestion accentuating mode of 'taxis are an essential mode of movement in [Kohima]' (GoI, 2017). As suggested earlier, an adequate supply of PTS in quantity (especially to cater to the un-served areas) as well as in quality (especially to induce a shift away from congestion accentuating private cars and taxis to congestion easing PTS) is therefore urgently imperative.

Excess Demand Over Supply of Transport

It emerges from the foregoing discussion that the observed severe traffic congestion in Kohima is primarily owing to a situation of demand exceeding supply. While the demand for transport is on the rise, the supply of transport – road capacity as well as PTS – has remained inadequate as well as inefficient, with neither quantity nor quality enhancement. Concomitantly, the mushrooming of private cars on the largely stagnant road capacity as well as parking capacity is worsening the already severely congested streets of the city (particularly along the central street). Accentuating the same is also the absence of an integrated spatial-building-transport strategy. While the ongoing ribbon development[3] of commerce along the central road of the city further accentuates congestion – as shoppers congregate along the same for shopping, the congestion in turn disrupts movement between the northern half and the southern half of the linear city (GoN, 2006), generating an economic cost as well as an ecological cost (as stated earlier).

Congestion Mitigation Model

Against the stated context of a rising demand for transport against a stagnant supply, traffic congestion mitigation is discussed in the following by employing a form of demand and supply analysis grounded on the concepts elucidated earlier. To begin with, however, the precincts of the model are outlined.

Limitations of the Model

The current analysis is different from econometric studies concerning estimation of elasticity – of income and of price by employing either primary or secondary data (of either time series or cross-sectional nature[4]) – that provides a critical evidence specifically for demand side management (for such a study, see Pirotte et al., 2011). An econometric analysis of congestion mitigation in the context of Kohima employing a primary data (of cross-sectional nature) is made in the next chapter. The model presented in the following is constructed sans certain micro-foundations such as price elasticity, income elasticity and commuters' behaviour (such as giving attention to a consideration of convenience). It does not also consider cases of the nature of conspicuous consumption. It is not, however, denied that such an aspect (and other aspirational reasons) provides an explanation to the increasing ownership of personnel cars to an extent.

The model is developed bearing in mind the stated idiosyncrasies characterizing traffic congestion in Kohima. Given such contextual specificities, it is aimed to demonstrate that non-pricing supply side mitigation should precede pricing as well as regulatory demand side mitigation for reasons explored within the discussion of the model. It is not, however, intended to scrutinize the efficacy of either the pricing instruments in practice or the regulatory practices to ease congestion in the context of Kohima.

Congestion Mitigation

As alluded to earlier, a form of demand and supply analysis is employed in a graphical model of congestion mitigation (in terms of Figure 5.2). In Figure 5.2, while the x-axis represents the number of commuters (T), the y-axis represents cost of commuting (g). Alongside, while the demand curves for travel [DD (travel) as well as DD' (travel)] are taken to be downward sloping (suggesting a negative relationship between cost of commuting and demand for travel), the extended congestion cost functions (as elucidated

Commuting Cost (g)

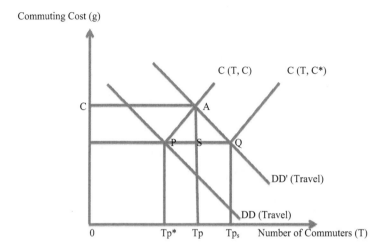

Figure 5.2 Congestion mitigation.

earlier) [C (T, C) as well as C (T, C*)] are taken to be upward sloping. The negative slope of the demand curve per se suggests the probable effectiveness of pricing measures to mitigate congestion – for a certain share of demand for travel can be decreased by increasing commuting cost, and thereby easing congestion to an equivalent extent corresponding to such a share of the decreased demand. The current concern is not, however, with the question of effectiveness of such pricing measures. The concern is, as stated earlier, with the question as to, *which should precede which*, supply side (or non-pricing) or demand side (or pricing as well as command and control) interventions, given the idiosyncrasies of a given context.

An equilibrium number of commuters is attained at an intersection between a demand curve and a supply curve (expressly, congestion cost curve). To begin with, we assume an initial condition where Kohima's traffic speed is at an optimum sans a congestion. Since such an optimum – represented by point P in figure 5.2 – is taken at the point of inflection beyond which congestion externality sets in, the extended congestion cost function can also be construed as a MC curve (and therefore, as cost of congestion from societal perspective). It may be recalled that an extended congestion cost function is a mirror image of an extended speed function – implying that when a traffic congestion (measured in traffic speed metric) increases, commuting cost also correspondingly increases (owing to an increase in congestion cost), and vice versa.

To proceed further, we now assume that a shift in the demand curve for transport occurs from DD to DD′ in figure 5.2 – as in the case of Kohima for multiple factors cited earlier. Consequently, the *pre-capacity expansion* extended congestion cost curve, C (T, C), intersects the shifted demand curve, DD', at point A, at which the corresponding number of commuters is Tp. Tp is, however, beyond the congestion-free extent of commuter threshold, Tp*, and therefore, congestion emerges owing to the same – the quantum of which is represented by Tp*Tp extent of marginal commuters.

A policy implication from the discussion so far is the necessity of an antic-ipatory urban mobility planning. The transport policy of France is an example of the same – involving drawing up of a master plan by updating a quinquen-nial long-run traffic forecast for enhancing road capacity (Pirotte and Madre, 2011). In the case of India, a major constraint for such a supply side enhance-ment is an insufficiency of financial resource (Rao and Rao, 2012).

Coming back to figure 5.2, in order to mitigate the aforesaid emergent con-gestion, Tp*Tp, market-based congestion pricing instruments will resort to *charges* (say, congestion tax) equivalent to an area marked PAS in figure 5.2 (or less) on the commuters using *prima facie* congestion-causing private cars (in order to cause a reduction in the number of commuters back to the congestion-free quantum, Tp*). Assuming the *charge* to be PAS, however, a deadweight loss (loosely means welfare loss to the society) equivalent to an area marked QAS in figure 5.2 arises.

The rationale for such a *pricing approach* is to reduce commuters using private cars by means of a substitution effect (substituting private cars with PTS). In the absence of a *substitute* (quantitatively as well as qualitatively adequate PTS), however, such an approach may only engender a loss of wel-fare. In terms of figure 5.2, a loss of welfare equivalent to PAS arises for commuters. In perspective, if the commuters using private cars for want of PTS are charged, such commuters are either *priced off the road* or bear an extra cost, which results in a loss of welfare. Such a loss of welfare is over and above the opportunity cost of income incurred as a result of the earning time wasted in congestion – which, in the context of Kohima, for more or less stagnant capacity (largely owing to policy failure), as discussed earlier. A similar effect of loss of welfare will be observed even if an authority, by means of *command and control*, reduces the number of commuters back to Tp* from Tp.

A classic counter argument is often advanced arguing that such a welfare loss is actually not a loss for an authority gains in revenue from the *charges*, which can be employed to finance economic development. Given the acute deficiency of the *substitute*, and 'transportation [being] an input to [almost] all urban activities' (Mohanty, 2014), however, the potential adverse impact on the wider economy and thereby on government revenue may neutralize such development potential.

In the context of Kohima, moreover, the question of propriety in charging commuters for *prima facie* failure of authority cannot be evaded. A *political challenge* as well as a compliance challenge may be therefore encountered if a *substitute* is not put in place beforehand. The *odd-even vehicle rationing scheme* of the government of Delhi – alternately allowing vehicles with odd and even registration numbers to ply on roads on alternate days – was reportedly not received well by the citizens, notwithstanding the emergency of severe ambient air pollution, citing the deficiency of an adequate PTS as a major reason. Furthermore, the limitations of congestion pricing (such as arising from heterogeneity of commuters, interactions of urban transport with the wider economy, and social as well as political resistance) as noted by Lindsey and Verhoef (2000) are more pronounced in cities of developing countries such as India. Above all, such an approach is in conflict to the stated imperative (in the preceding part II of the book) of an integrated urban planning that concurrently considers the concerns of an inclusive growth as well as a salubrious environment.

Having said so, in a situation where congestion is primarily a consequence of an inadequate supply, it is more efficient, more equitable as well as more pragmatic to initially invest in capacity expansion. In figure 5.2, after capacity expansion – indicated by a shift of the extended cost function from C (T, C) to C (T, C*), the congestion-free threshold of an extent of commuters extends from Tp* to Tp_s. If the aforesaid arisen congestion, Tp*Tp, is mitigated entirely through an urban mobility capacity expansion, neither loss of welfare nor deadweight loss emerge – as is evident from the diagram. At least in theory, such a loss is zero. Furthermore, such a supply side intervention engenders 'accessibility and serviceability premiums locally [as well as] wider economic benefits to the whole economy by enhancing access . . . leading to agglomeration and network economies while mitigating congestion diseconomies' (Panda et al., 2020). Analogously, 'endogenous growth [models] suggest [that] infrastructure can act as a powerful driver of growth by impacting knowledge externalities' (Panda et al., 2020).

For financial, environmental as well as other associated opportunity cost rationales, however, a continual complete alleviation of congestion by means of such an expansion in capacity is unpragmatic. The necessity to employ pricing instruments thereby arises. The same further implies that neither a loss of welfare nor a deadweight loss can be reduced to zero in practice. Be that as it may, however, if such a demand side intervention is preceded by a supply side intervention to the extent pragmatic, such a loss can be correspondingly minimized to the same extent.

In terms of figure 5.2, even if an expansion of capacity of a scale smaller than that necessitated by the shifted demand (represented by an imaginary in-between extended congestion cost function – not shown in figure 5.2 – between C (T, C), the pre-capacity expansion cost function, and C (T, C*), the post-capacity expansion cost function), it can be ascertained that after the said expansion of capacity, even if the demand is brought down to an equilibrium quantum corresponding to the in-between congestion cost function by means of either a congestion pricing or a command and control, a welfare loss as well as a deadweight loss are minimized. It may be argued that such a welfare loss as well as a deadweight loss can be minimized to the same extent by partially shifting down the demand curve to an equivalent extent either through pricing or through command and control. In that case, however, the problems associated with an absence of *substitute* (of the nature discussed earlier) will not be addressed. An approach of such a nature may therefore escalate mobility cost as well as engender an adverse bearing on economic growth.

The traditional supply side approach of enhancing road capacity is subjected to the established paradoxes in Transport Economics – Piguo-Knight-Downs paradox, Downs-Thomson paradox and Braess paradox – suggesting a paradoxical outcome following such an enhancement in capacity, and thereby rendering such intervention either ineffective or even counter-productive (for empirical evidence of the same, see Arnott and Kenneth, 1994). (While Piguo-Knight-Downs paradox suggests that a road capacity expansion induces a new demand for travel resulting in either no improvement or even worsening of congestion on the same road, Downs-Thomson paradox suggests that a road capacity expansion diverts commuters from other roads to the expanded road resulting in either no improvement or even worsening of congestion on the same road, and Braess Paradox suggests that adding a new link causes travel time to increase.) The consequently inevitable requirement of demand side management is suggested owing to such paradoxical results. In order to minimize the loss of the stated nature, however, such a demand side intervention should be made only after a supply side intervention to the extent pragmatic – or only after putting in place the *substitute*. It is neither suggested to solely eliminate *congestion by constructing roads;* nor by supply side intervention, road capacity expansion is exclusively suggested (as discussed in the following). Above all, such paradoxes are not to be cited by an authority as justification to abdicate provisioning of an adequate capacity.

On the supply side, an immediately imperative intervention is, as mentioned earlier, a 'provision of bus services of a quality that would be acceptable to [commuters] currently using private transport' (Ahluwalia and Mohanty, 2014). On the demand side, an accompanying intervention to strengthen the outcome of the supply side intervention is a nudging scheme (by means of information dissemination – as discussed in Part II of the book – or suchlike) to shift preferences of commuters away from congestion-causing cars towards congestion easing PTS. Of note, the small-scale voluntary citizens' initiatives to ease congestion (of the nature of *Cars Free Thursdays* in Hyderabad) can be leveraged and institutionalized for such initiatives tend to be mostly sporadic. An outcome of such a combined intervention – an increase in the number of commuters per lane hour – is equivalent to an expansion of road capacity (and the concomitant easing of congestion as well as the further follow-on reduction in vehicular pollution).

Given the practicality problem of green non-motorized modes (such as walking and cycling) owing to the hilly terrain of Kohima, PTS assumes an even greater salience in the city. In order to minimize the adverse bearing on economic growth in the pursuit of an ecological concern (expressly, reduction of vehicular pollution by easing congestion), and in accordance with the argument made in the previous part II (expressly, the desirability of a growing economy as well as a salubrious environment), congestion pricing ought to be effected only after putting in place the *substitute* of PTS. Moreover, PTS will 'provide better service to the lower-income groups that tend to patronize it. Also, the wealthy are likely to benefit from being able to buy uncongested road space, a situation they value because of the importance they attach to time savings' (Button, 2010). Such a provision of PTS is therefore of prime salience to the core elements of sustainable development – economic growth, environmental protection and social inclusion.

Along with the recommendations made in passing in the previous section on the measures to be effected on the supply side (such as efficient road design, enhancement of parking capacity as well as efficient parking policy, and provision of bus station as well as truck terminal), other suchlike measures should also be effected in Kohima. That traffic accidents take place owing to reckless driving as well (GoN, 2006) suggests shortcomings in the extant Traffic Management System (TMS). Along with a capacity enhancement of the traffic personnel, therefore, an Intelligent Traffic Management System (ITMS) should be operationalized. All such measures extend the congestion-free commuter threshold – in terms of figure 5.2, moving Tp* further rightward – and thereby either delays the setting in of congestion or reduces the prevailing congestion.

To end with, an investment in urban mobility system is immediately imperative in order to leverage the potential of Kohima to propel the state's as well as the region's economic growth. An efficient urban mobility system not only widens and deepens labour market (thereby augmenting the productivity of workers) but also balances employment and housing – further generating a value increment to either refund an already developed infrastructure (say, with credit) or fund a new urban infrastructure. An investment in such a system engenders accessibility premium (by means of facilitating development of land for productive uses) and wider economic benefits (Graham, 2007; Graham and Gibbon, 2018; Venables, 2007; Vickerman, 2008). By enhancing accessibility, investment in the same augments agglomeration economies, reduces congestion diseconomies and channelizes economic growth in desired direction.

Conclusion

Given the contextual specificities of traffic congestion in Kohima, an extended speed function and an extended cost function (as opposed to the standard speed function and cost function) – as elucidated earlier – are better suited to make a demand and supply analysis of the city's urban mobility.

Given the nature of traffic congestion in Kohima, wherein an increasing demand for transport exceeds a stagnating supply of transport, resorting to either congestion pricing or command and control is not the apposite initial approach for mitigating the same, for rationales connected to welfare as well as practicality. Considering that no singular measure is sufficient in addressing the same, however, supply side measures should precede such demand side measures. The provision of quantitatively as well as qualitatively adequate PTS is in particular immediately imperative for a sustainable mobility. Such a sustainable urban transport will contribute to making Kohima a green engine of growth.

Notes

1 Elasticity measures the degree of responsiveness of a variable (say, gasoline demand) to a change in another variable (say, price of gasoline).
2 An Equivalent Car Space for a vehicle other than a car is calculated in relation to a parking slot dimension of a car (5 m × 2 m) taken as 1.
3 Ribbon development contextually refers to the development of commercial establishments alongside the central road of Kohima.
4 While time series data involves measurements (or observations) about subject(s) over a period of time, cross-sectional data involves measurements about subject(s) at a particular point of time.

References

Ahluwalia, Mathur and Mohanty, P K, *Urbanisation in India: challenges, opportunities and the way forward*. Sage, New Delhi, 2014.
Alam, Absar M and Ahmed, Faisal, *Urban transport systems and congestion: a case study of Indian cities*. Transport and Communications Bulletin for Asia and the Pacific, No. 82, 33–43, 2013.
Arnott, Richard and Kenneth, Small, *The Economics of Traffic Congestion*. American Scientist, 82, 446–455, 1994.
Button, Kenneth, *Transport economics*. Edward Elgar Publishing Limited, The Lypiatts, 2010.
Dzuvichu, L, *Roads and the raj: the politics of road building in colonial Naga Hills, 1860s–1910s*. The Indian Economic and Social History Review, 50(4), 473–494, 2013.
Government of India, *Census of India*. Government of India, 2011. http://censusindia.gov.in/
Government of India, *Kohima smart city proposal*. Government of India, 2017. http://smartcities.gov.in/
Government of Nagaland, *City Development Plan*. www.nagaland.gov.in/, 2006.
Government of Nagaland, *District Human Development Report – Kohima*. Government of Nagaland, 2009. www.in.undp.org/
Government of Nagaland, *Nagaland state human development report*. Government of Nagaland, 2004. www.in.undp.org/
Government of Nagaland, *Nagaland Vision 2030*. Government of Nagaland, 2016. www.nagaland.gov.in/

Government of Nagaland, *Statistical handbook of Nagaland*. N V Press, Kohima, 2014.

Government of Nagaland, *Statistical handbook of Nagaland*. N V Press, Kohima, 2022.

Graham, D J, *Agglomeration, productivity and transport investment*. Journal of Transport Economics and Policy, 41, 1–27, 2007.

Graham, D J and Gibbons, S, *Quantifying wide economic impacts of agglomeration for transport appraisal: existing evidence and future directions*. CEP Discussion Paper No 1561, 1–21, 2018.

Hughes, J, Knittel, C and Sperling, D, *Evidence of a shift in the short-run price elasticity of gasoline demand*. Energy Journal, 29(1), 113–134, 2008. https://doi.org/10.5547/0195-6574-EJ-Vol29-No1-9

Humtsoe, Tumbenthung Y, *From pathways to roadways: issues and challenges of road transport in Nagaland*. Growth and Change, 1–20, 2020. https://doi.org/10.1111/grow.12383

Humtsoe, Tumbenthung Y, *Travel mode choice in the North-eastern Indian city of Kohima: lessons from empirical study*. Journal of Urbanism: International Research on Placemaking and Urban Sustainability, 2022. https://doi.org/10.1080/17549175.2022.2041465

Kire, Easterine, *Mari*. Harper Collins Publisher, India, 2010.

Lindsey, Robin C and Verhoef, Erik T, *Traffic congestion and congestion pricing*. Tinbergen Institute Discussion Paper, 2000. https://research.vu.nl/

Mishra, A K, *Cities, transport and agglomeration: addressing the urban mobility challenges in India*. Growth and Change, 1–19, 2019. https://doi.org/10.1111/grow.12321

Mohanty, P K, *Cities and public policy: an urban agenda for India*. Sage India, New Delhi, 2014.

Nagaland Board of School Education, *A book on Nagaland*. N V. Press, Kohima, 2015.

Nagaland Pollution Control Board, *Air Monitoring*. Nagaland Pollution Control Board, 2016. https://npcb.nagaland.gov.in

North Eastern Council, Government of India, *Basic statistics of North Eastern Region*. North Eastern Council, 2015. https://necouncil.gov.in/

Panda, Prerna, Mishra, Alok Kumar and Mishra, Shibani, *Externalities and urban infrastructure financing: a new theoretical model and lessons for smart cities in India*. International Journal of Transport Economics, xlvi(1), 51–74, 2020.

Pirotte, Alain and Madre, Jean-Loup, *Car traffic elasticities: a spatial panel data analysis of French regions*. Journal of Transport Economics and Policy, 45(3), pp. 341–365, 2011.

Rao, Amudapuram Mohan and Rao, Kalaga Ramachandra, *Measuring urban traffic congestion – a review*. International Journal for Traffic and Transport Engineering, 2(4), 286–305, 2012.

Small, K A and Dender, Van K, *Fuel efficiency and motor vehicle travel: the declining rebound effect*. Energy Journal, 28(1), 25–51, 2007. https://doi.org/10.5547/0195-6574-EJ-Vol28-No1-2

Venables, A J, *Evaluating urban transport improvements: cost – benefit analysis in the presence of agglomeration and income taxation*. Journal of Transport Economics and Policy, 41, 173–188, 2007.

Vickerman, R, *Transit investment and economic development*. Research in Transportation Economics, 23, 107–115, 2008. https://doi.org/10.1016/j.retrec.2008.10.007

Yedla, Sudhakar, *Non-motorized modes of transport in urban transportation and the environment*. Springer, New Delhi, 2015. https://doi.org/10.1007/978-81-322-2313-9_5

6 Empirical Lessons for Sustainable Urban Mobility

Introduction

As mentioned earlier, urban mobility across developing economies is not without challenges at present. The imperative for managing such concerns cannot be overstated, especially to leverage the ongoing urbanization as a green resource (as explicated earlier). By employing secondary data, urban mobility challenges in the context of Kohima, a highland city at the frontier, have been discussed in the preceding chapter 5. More of such concerns are discussed in the present chapter by means of primary statistics.

As stated in the preceding chapter 5, traffic congestion can be mitigated either solely through supply side management (SSM) or solely through demand side management (DSM), or through a combination of the same. What emerges strongly from the literature surveyed in the preceding chapter 5 is that an appropriate shifting of a commuting behaviour away from congestion accentuating modes towards congestion easing modes requires neither only SSM nor only DSM (nor only a combination of the same) as in practice, which does not incorporate views of commuters. For effective congestion mitigation, feasible inputs from the commuters should be incorporated in SSM as well as DSM to bring about consumer-relevant developments in urban mobility. It is therefore envisaged in the current chapter to provide preliminary and original evidence towards addressing the said limitation.

By employing primary data, an econometric model of travel mode choice for the citizens of Kohima is constructed in order to further contribute towards an evidence-informed (and thereby more effective) sustainable urban mobility development and management strategy in the highland city.

Data and Sampling Strategy

The study employs primary statistics by means of an *urban transport sample survey* conducted in Kohima. The sample is proportionately drawn from each of the 19 spatially demarcated municipal election wards (GoI, 2011) according to the census population percentage of each ward (as shown in Table 6.1).

DOI: 10.4324/9781032711799-9

Table 6.1 Sampling strategy

Ward Number	Total Population	Percentage	Number of Respondents
0001	7082	7.15	18
0002	5207	5.25	13
0003	5692	5.74	8
0004	3568	3.60	9
0005	3197	3.22	9
0006	5381	5.43	14
0007	2721	2.75	9
0008	2348	2.38	8
0009	4808	4.85	12
0010	4820	4.86	12
0011	5267	5.31	13
0012	3848	3.88	10
0013	3228	3.26	9
0014	6101	6.16	16
0015	7970	8.04	20
0016	11,603	11.72	30
0017	7775	7.85	19
0018	4809	4.86	12
0019	3614	3.64	9
Total	99,039	100	250

Source: GoI (2011) and author's calculation

While making the sample representative, such a sampling design reflects as well as captures the critical salience of space (expressly, locations) in the generation of demand for travel. By means of structured as well as unstructured and open-ended interviews, as mentioned in Chapter 1, information (including unconventional yet pertinent responses) are randomly gathered altogether from 250 households on the following parameters: socio-economic profile of household, characteristics of automobile use (under which certain questions are directed only to owners of cars), trip statistics, quality of bus service, traffic congestion and air pollution.

Basic Particulars of Household Members

To a considerable extent, a socio-economic profile of an economic agent (as well as of a household) influences the economic decisions of an agent. To begin with, such basic particulars of household members in Kohima are accordingly given in Table 6.2. Suggestive of the absence of female foeticide and infanticide in the state as a whole, a largely even sex ratio is registered in Kohima – with male constituting about 49%, while female comprising about 51%. Reflective of Kohima as a centre of education, while a majority of the population are students, the population is reasonably educated as well – with a majority having a graduate degree. Again, indicative of Kohima as a centre of administration, maximum workforce is engaged in government sector – which is also telling of the underdeveloped private sector in the capital as well as in the state. The average monthly household income of ₹35,104 should be considered bearing in mind the high standard deviation[1] value of 19.65 (see Table 6.3), which may be explained from the high degree of disparity in the size of income corresponding to the different occupations of the population. While further particulars apropos gender, marital status, educational level and occupation are presented in Table 6.2, particulars apropos age are presented

Table 6.2 Gender, marital status, educational status and occupation

Parameter	Category	Percentage	Cumulative Frequency
Gender	Male	48.9	48.9
	Female	51.1	100
Marital status	Married	37.91	37.91
	Unmarried	62.08	100
Educational status	No schooling	1.8	1.8
	Primary (up to Class 5)	9.02	10.82
	High school (up to Class 10)	21.25	32.07
	Higher secondary (up to Class 12)	22.36	54.43
	Graduate	34.02	88.45
	Masters	11.52	100
Occupation	Unemployed	11.94	11.94
	Government employee	24.86	36.8
	Pensioner	2.63	39.43
	Working professional in private sector	13.05	52.48
	Own business	6.66	59.14
	Daily wage	0.27	59.41
	Student	32.77	92.18
	Housewife	7.77	100

Source: Author's calculation

Table 6.3 Age and income

Variable	Mean[1]	Std. Dev.
Age (in years)	31	14.47
Income (in ₹)	35,104	19.65

Source: Author's calculation

[1] Mean is average in statistics.

in Table 6.3. Again, although the rather young average age of the population at 31 years should be considered bearing in mind the high standard deviation value of 14.47, the same is reflective of the agglomeration of students, civil service exam aspirants and other suchlike young job seekers – thereby also creating a potential for demographic dividend.

Trip Information

As can be gleaned from Table 6.4, a largely even distribution exists in the modes of travel. In what is a stark contrast to other cities of India, the share of *two-wheeler* in Kohima is insignificant (about 1%) – as compared to the significant share of two-wheeler in India (about 74% in 2015) (GoI, 2018). Using a two-wheeler is practically undesirable to an extent in Kohima for climatic as well as infrastructural reasons. During the long monsoon season, Kohima – along with the rest of the NER – receives an extremely heavy average rainfall. During the winter season, while the climate is cold, the insufficiently maintained urban roads are dusty.

Given the existing even distribution in the modes of travel, while it is necessary to maximize the share of congestion easing modes of travel (bus and walking), it is necessary to minimize the share of congestion accentuating modes of travel (car as well as taxi).

As can be understood from Table 6.4 again, the generators of trips are in accordance with the demographic profile of Kohima. Accordingly, work/office as well as school/colleges account for the maximum generators of trips. For congestion mitigation, the generation of trips requiring congestion accentuating modes of travel for such purposes should be minimized to the extent pragmatic (as suggested earlier, through an integrated land use–transport urban policy and suchlike). Of note, the observed easing of congestion in the otherwise congested main street of Kohima whenever offices are closed suggests the probable effectiveness of congestion mitigation by

Table 6.4 Travel modes and trip purposes

Variable	Category	Percentage	Cumulative Frequency
Mode of travel	Car	23.02	23.02
	Bus	29.94	52.96
	Taxi	20.19	73.15
	Walking	26.12	99.27
	Two-wheeler	0.7	100
Trip purpose	Office/Work	34.74	34.74
	School/Colleges	34.18	68.92
	Social visits	20.33	89.25
	Marketing	10.73	100

Source: Author's calculation

Table 6.5 Trip distance, trip time, trip cost and fuel expenditure

Variable	Mean	Std. Dev.	Min	Max
Trip distance (in km)	2.82	2.82	0.1 (100 m)	20
Trip time (in min)	28.9	27.86	1	180
Trip cost (in ₹)	46.40	26.52	0	250
Monthly fuel expenditure (in ₹)	2881	28.56	2000	5000

Source: Author's calculation

means of reducing such a demand for conveyance for work (by means of an integrated urban policy or otherwise).

As can be ascertained from Table 6.5, on a single trip, a typical commuter in Kohima – on an average – commutes for around 3 km in about 30 min and incurs around ₹46. As mentioned earlier in chapter 5, suggesting an accentuation of traffic congestion, the traffic speed in Kohima decreased from about 13 km/h to about 6 km/h (as can be worked out from the stated information) in about a decade's time. A zero cost in the case of walking on the one hand and a high cost in the case of taking a taxi – which is reported to increase even higher in an event (as well as in an area) of unavailability of bus service – on the other hand explain to an extent the high standard deviation value of *trip cost*. The high standard deviation value of *monthly fuel expenditure* is similarly explained to an extent by the comparatively low fuel expenditure by cars on the one hand and the relatively high fuel expenditure by taxis on the other hand. As suggested in the previous chapter 5, an adequate supply of PTS in quantity (especially to cater to the un-served areas) as well as in quality (especially to induce a shift away from congestion accentuating private cars and taxis to congestion easing PTS) is urgently imperative.

Characteristics of Automobile Use

As reported in Table 6.6, about 56% of the households own at least a single vehicle, with a comparable percentage of about 44% owning none. With respect to the respondents, while about 45% are owners of vehicles, about 55% are not. That the supply of PTS is grossly inadequate – and thereby conveyance arrangement is mostly *own arrangement* – can be understood from the nature of automobile ownership in Kohima as well. Automobiles are almost wholly *privately owned* (95%), with *organization owned* (almost wholly government owned) comprising merely about 5%. Of the nature of automobiles, *cars* comprise about 92%. Such an extremely high per capita ownership of car (as suggested in the preceding chapter 5 as well as reflected in the data presented in the following, augmented by a thriving used-car market in the

Table 6.6 Household automobile ownership

Number of Cars per Household	0	1	2	3	4	5 and More
Percentage	44.44	44.44	8.64	2.05	0	0.41
Cumulative frequency	44.44	88.88	97.52	99.57	99.57	100

Source: Author's calculation

Table 6.7 Characteristics of automobile use and alternative modes of commuting

Variables	Category	Percentage	Cumulative Frequency
Age of cars (in years)	Less than 5 years	53.84	53.84
	Between 5 and 10 years	35.89	89.73
	Between 10 and 15 years	2.56	92.29
	15 years and more	7.69	100
Whether purchased new or used cars	New	81.9	81.9
	Used	18.10	100
Alternative mode in case of unavailability of cars	Someone else's car	1.98	1.98
	Bus	33.11	35.09
	Taxi	47.01	82.1
	Walk	8.6	90.7
	Work from home	0.66	91.36
	Bike	8.6	100
Cited factors for the alternative mode	Easy accessibility	26.05	26.05
	Cheaper cost	19.32	45.37
	Convenience and comfort	34.45	79.82
	Unavailability of bus service	2.52	82.34
	Health	5.04	87.38
	Reliability of reaching on time	3.36	90.74
	Safety	5.88	96.62
	Traffic jam	2.52	99.14
	Environmental concerns (energy, GHG and other pollutants)	0.84	100

Source: Author's calculation

state) inter alia spells the salience of demand side intervention (however, the same should be preceded by supply side intervention for rationales cited in the preceding chapter 5). Henceforth, cars will be therefore used interchangeably with automobiles.

As can be gleaned from Table 6.7, concerning the *age of cars*, most of the cars are less than 10 years, and are purchased *brand new*. Considering that an age of a car has an implication on air pollution, however, it is still a concern to note that while about 8% of the cars are either 15 years of age or more, about 18% of the cars are purchased as used cars. In case of unavailability of *car* mode, the preferred alternative mode of travel for most of the car owners is *taxi*. The factor mostly cited while choosing such an alternative mode is *convenience and comfort*. Again, a policy implication that arises from the same is a quantitatively as well as qualitatively adequate supply of PTS. More aspects on the quality of bus service are discussed in the ensuing section. Above all, that an environmental concern is not considered while choosing an alternative mode (with only less than 1% reporting such a consideration) spells the immediate imperative of an environmental awareness dissemination (the salience of which is also emphasized in the preceding part II of the book).

Bus Transit Information and Quality of Bus Service

As reported in Table 6.8, while a negligible percentage of the respondents does not avail bus service, a majority avails bus service *several times in a week* as well as *in a month*. An availability of *bus stop* within a walkable distance is, however, far from ideal. For almost 29% of the respondents, no bus stop

Table 6.8 Bus transit information and quality of bus service

Variables	Category	Percentage	Cumulative Frequency
How often do you take a bus?	Not at all	2.1	2.1
	Daily	21.09	23.19
	Several times a week	38.39	61.58
	Several times a month	29.11	90.69
	Few times in a year	9.28	100
How many bus stops within a *walkable* **distance?**	0	28.95	28.95
	1	40.72	69.67
	2	27.6	97.27
	3	2.26	99.53
	4 and more	0.45	100
Is bus service frequency sufficient?	Yes	54.43	54.43
	No	45.56	100
Is bus fare expensive?	Yes	30.83	30.83
	No	69.16	100
How about cleanliness inside a bus?	Good	30.83	30.83
	Bad	69.16	100
Does commuting by a bus take too long?	Yes	60.66	60.66
	No	39.33	100
Are there too many transfers?	Yes	32.35	32.35
	No	67.64	100
Is commuting by a bus safe?	Yes	87.02	87.02
	No	12.97	100
Is commuting by a bus comfortable?	Yes	53.36	53.36
	No	46.63	100
Compared to previous year, how would you rate the bus service quality?	Improved	9.36	9.36
	Remained the same	66.38	75.74
	Worsened	11.06	86.8
	Don't know	13.19	100

Source: Author's calculation

Table 6.9 Bus stop information

Variable	Mean	Std. Dev.	Min	Max
Time spend walking to a bus stop (in min)	9.95	7.17	1	33
Time spend waiting for a bus (in min)	5.32	4.16	0 (less than 1 min)	20

Source: Author's calculation

exists within a walkable reach from home. Consequently, a respondent – on an average – spends about 10 min walking to a bus stop, where it takes about 5 min to board a bus (see Table 6.9) – suggesting that *bus service frequency* is more or less sufficient. Accordingly, about 54% considers bus service frequency *sufficient*.

As reported in Table 6.8 again, around 69% of the respondents do not find bus fare *expensive* – suggesting a scope for improving the quality of bus service even if the same entails an increase in bus fare to an extent. That such a quality enhancement is immediately imperative can be ascertained from the responses on the existing quality aspects of bus service. A majority of about 53% considers commuting by bus *not comfortable*. Analogously, a staggeringly 69% regards *cleanliness of bus* as *bad*. Of a more concern is that a majority of about 66% observes that the *bus service quality remained about the same* over the preceding year – suggesting no signs of progress in quality.

Given the extant traffic congestion (as well as an absence of a bus way), around 60% considers that *commuting by bus takes too long*. Only about 32%, however, reports that *too many transfers of bus* exist. A too long in commuting time by bus in spite of not too many transfers of bus further corroborates the slow traffic speed in Kohima. On an aspect with a bearing on empowerment of women (as well as children) – and thereby on the inclusiveness constituent of sustainable mobility, however, commuting by bus is perceived to be *safe*.

Adverse Impacts From Reduced Bus Service

Commuting by bus forms a basic necessity of the day-to-day socio-economic activities of many individuals in a city, especially for the LIG. The quality of bus service therefore significantly impacts the quality of urban life – more so when a bus service is the sole available mode of PTS. As reported in Table 6.10, in an event of either reduced or no bus service at all, about 59% of the respondents report a *loss of time*, and further adds that in such an event, 'are often late to either workplace or schools and colleges.' In an event of either reduced availability or unavailability of the most affordable mode of conveyance, bus service, the demand for the then only available mode, taxi, exceeds the supply, creating a higher fare of the latter. Accordingly, about 28% reports incurring a higher cost of conveyance in such an event. An additional

Table 6.10 Impacts from reduced or no bus service

Variables	Category	Percentage	Cumulative Frequency
What are the impacts from reduced or no bus service?	Inconvenience	4.61	4.61
	Increase in cost	28.46	33.07
	Loss of time	59.23	92.3
	No effect	7.69	100
Will you use bus on Sunday?	Yes	82.70	82.70
	No	17.29	100

Source: Author's calculation

transaction cost – walking to a taxi stand as well as negotiating a fare – is also involved. Such an increase in the fare of taxi is, however, not to be mistaken to imply a necessity to increase the supply of taxi (which would further accentuate the already severe congestion). Instead, the supply of bus, a congestion easing mode, is to be increased. Of note, a reduction in the existing number of taxis is suggested by the respondents in order to ease congestion, and to accelerate the speed of bus transit (as shall be seen later). If a bus service is provided on Sundays (on which days such a service is currently unavailable), about 83% responds to avail the same – further corroborating the necessity of expanding the same.

Suggestions for Enhancing Bus Service Quality

Incorporating inputs from consumers is imperative in order to bring about consumer-relevant enhancement in the quality of either products or services. In accordance with the reasonably educated population of Kohima, a set of informed as well as ingenious suggestions of bus service quality enhancement is advanced by the same, from which policy makers can profitably extract. The following are the recurring suggestions presented in a decreasing order of frequency of response: (i) more capacious as well as cleaner buses, (ii) specified shuttle schedule adhering to strict punctuality, (iii) extending bus services to un-served areas[2] by increasing the number of bus (preferably by the government), (iv) enhancing the ride quality of bus by enhancing the quality of road, (v) restructuring the extant fare system according to distance travelled, (vi) provisioning adequate parking space,[3] including for buses, (vii) strict regulation of quality by authority including checking of behaviour of drivers as well as conductors, (viii) mitigating traffic congestion in order to increase the speed of conveyance by bus – including by means of reducing the number of private taxis as well as private cars, (ix) provisioning a bus way, (x) providing a *bus card* system, (xi) provisioning bus service sans transfers between distant neighbourhoods, (xii) providing bus service at night, (xiii) enforcing no smoking as well as no chewing of tobacco inside a bus, (xiv) disseminating awareness on the gains of using PTS, (xv) mandating transparent window on a bus in order to enhance the ride quality in terms of window viewing as well as safety, and (xvi) finally, a well-trained traffic police.

Given the many supply side constraints in the extant state of urban mobility in Kohima (as discussed in the previous chapter 5), the suggestions advanced are expectedly of the nature of supply side intervention.

Traffic Congestion and Vehicular Air Pollution

As reported in Table 6.11, in accordance with what is already said about the severe traffic congestion in Kohima, while about 50% of the respondents report that the state of congestion is either *very bad* or *severe*, around 28% observes the same to be *bad*. Given the proliferation of cars on a more or less stagnant road capacity, almost all the respondents (about 95%) opine that traffic volume is in excess of the road carrying capacity. The observed severe congestion is therefore only expected.

The salience of information in the form of *environmental awareness* in generating demand for more environmental goods (or higher quantum of environmental improvement) is well established. Strengthening the immediate necessity of disseminating environmental awareness to affect a desirable change in the commuting behaviour of an agent, a majority (around 58%) of the respondents was unaware of air pollution being above the safe norm in Kohima (see Table 6.11).

Moreover, on the one hand, suggesting an effectiveness of such an environmental strategy by coupling information propagation as well as quantitatively and qualitatively adequate PTS (as mentioned earlier), while about 76% responds that a parking charge is acceptable on environmental ground if quality PTS is available (see Table 6.12), around 45% registers a willingness to shift from car to bus on environmental ground, with another 32% responding to shift provided the quality of bus service improves (see Table 6.13). Almost all of the respondents (about 92%) report to take a bus more frequently if the quality of the same improves (see Table 6.13). To reiterate, an enhancement

Table 6.11 Traffic congestion and vehicular air pollution

Variable	Category	Percentage	Cumulative Frequency
How would you rate the existing state of congestion?	No problem	21.84	21.84
	Bad	27.73	49.57
	Very bad	23.52	73.09
	Severe	26.89	100
Are you aware of the above safe norm air pollution?	Yes	41.59	41.59
	No	58.40	100
Is traffic volume in excess of road capacity?	Yes	95.39	95.39
	No	4.61	100

Source: Author's calculation

Table 6.12 Parking charge

Variable	Category	Percentage	Cumulative Frequency
Is parking charge acceptable on environmental ground if PTS of quality is available?	Yes No	76.05 23.94	76.05 100
Is the prevailing parking charge expensive?	Yes No	61.29 38.71	61.29 100
Does parking charge discourage you from using car?	Yes No	44 56	44 100

Source: Author's calculation

Table 6.13 Shift from car to bus

Variable	Category	Percentage	Cumulative Frequency
Will you shift from car to bus on environmental ground?	Yes No If only the quality of bus service improves	45.45 22.72 31.81	45.45 68.17 100
Will you take a bus more frequently if the quality of bus service improves?	Yes No	92 8	92 100

Source: Author's calculation

of bus service quality is imperative to incentivise a change towards a more environmentally friendly bus mode of mobility.

On the other hand, suggesting a comparatively reduced effectiveness of pricing strategy, despite a majority (about 61%) considering the existing parking charge to be expensive, a majority (around 56%) responds that a parking charge is not a disincentive to car use (see Table 6.12). To be effective in mitigating congestion as well as pollution, a parking charge scheme should be therefore accompanied with a *nudging* scheme (as mentioned earlier, by means of an awareness drive and suchlike), including an incentive approach by making PTS a comparatively much more desirable mode.

Suggestions for Congestion Mitigation

Again, a set of informed as well as ingenious suggestions for congestion mitigation is advanced, which can be gainfully considered by policy makers. Concerning congestion mitigation, the following are the recurring suggestions presented in a decreasing order of frequency of response: (i) expansion of road capacity including a circular road, (ii) enhancement of PTS, (iii) provision of parking spaces in commercial areas, (iv) reduction in the number of private cars as well as taxis, (v) enhancement of traffic management, (vi) construction of flyovers,[4] (vii) promotion of walking mode, (viii) introduction of cable car, (ix) implementation of *odd and even vehicle rationing scheme* and other suchlike schemes, (x) relocation of some government offices outside of Kohima, (xi) establishment of educational institutions outside of Kohima, (xii) promotion of carpooling as well as taxi-sharing, (xiii) implementation of urban planning, (xiv) dissemination of awareness about vehicular air pollution owing to congestion, (xv) provision of footpath, pedestrian overpass and zebra crossing, (xvi) application of Intelligent Transport System (ITS), and (xvii) rationing of vehicle ownership per household.

Analogous to the suggestions for bus service quality enhancement, and as arrived from the analysis made in the preceding chapter 5, the suggestions advanced for congestion mitigation are initially of the nature of supply side intervention, followed by suggestions of the nature of demand side intervention.

Travel Mode Choice Model

What aspects may be associated with travel mode choice of an individual on any given time? From extant literature, such determining factors of travel mode choice can be categorized as follows. To begin with, a category of *socio economic and demographic characteristics*, which includes factors such as per capita income. Next, a category of *trip attributes*, which includes aspects such as cost of a particular transport mode. To end with, a category of *trip-related locational aspects*, which includes factors such as an existence of a bus stop within a walkable distance from a trip origin (Qin et al., 2013). Such a list of variables considered in an econometric model of travel mode choice for citizens of Kohima is presented in Table 6.14 (the descriptive statistics of the same are detailed in the preceding sections, and are therefore not repeated in the present section).

Given the binary nature of the regressand (the dependant variable, as explained in the following), and the regressors (the determining variables listed in Table 6.14, which influences the dependent variable) taking on dummy as well as categorical variables (qualitative variables such as gender and marital status), a logit model is employed to analyse a travel mode choice of an individual. As mentioned earlier, the model is conceived considering the severe traffic congestion in Kohima. The dependent variable (choices among alternative modes of mobility) is therefore binary, either a *congestion accentuating mode* or a *congestion easing mode*. Given the existing modes of urban mobility in Kohima, while the former includes private cars and *taxis*,[5] the latter includes walking, buses and taxi-sharing.[6] The logit function takes the following form:

$$\ln(p) - \ln(p - 1) = \beta_1 + \beta_1 X_1 \ldots \beta_n X_n$$

where $X_1, \ldots, X_n$ represent the regressors listed in Table 6.14.

Table 6.14 Variables

Sl. No.	Variable
1	Trip distance (in km)
2	Trip time (in min)
3	Trip cost (in ₹)
4	Age (in years)
5	Monthly income (in ₹)
6	Trip purpose
7	Gender
8	Relationship to head of family
9	Marital status
10	Educational status
11	Occupation
12	Number of cars in a household[1]

Source: Author

Discussion of Results

The estimation results presented in Table 6.15 is obtained by running the regression (to quantitatively estimate the relationship between the dependent variable and the independent variables) on statistical software, Eviews. A discussion of the result of the logit model is limited to the statistically significant variables (as shown in Table 6.15). (A statistically significant independent variable suggests that its relationship with a dependent variable is not by a chance alone.) Concerning socio-economic and demographic characteristics, the coefficient on *number of cars* is expectedly positive, suggesting an increase in the probability of choosing a congestion accentuating mode (expressly, car) with an increase in that variable. Apropos trip attributes, the coefficient of *trip time* and that of *trip cost* are expectedly negative – suggesting a decrease in the probability of choosing a particular mode (say, taxi) with an increase in the trip time variable (say, trip time by taxi) and with an increase in the trip cost variable (say, trip cost of taxi). Regarding trip-related locational aspects, even though the coefficient of a *bus stop within a walkable distance* is statistically insignificant (and therefore not shown in Table 6.15), the same is negative – suggesting a decrease in the probability of choosing a congestion easing mode (specifically, bus) with an increase in that variable. In other words, the probability of taking a bus increases with an increase in the availability of a bus stop within reach.

A policy implication that emerges from all this is that, while a congestion easing PTS that takes a reduced trip time as well as a reduced trip cost should be made available that can be accessed within a walkable distance, a congestion accentuating mode of car should be reduced by incorporating suggestions made earlier on the same (such as implementation of odd and even rationing of car, and rationing of car ownership per household).

Table 6.15 Statistically significant logit estimation results

Variable	Coefficient	Std. Error	z-Statistic	Prob.
AGE__IN_YEARS_	0.057687	0.010504	5.491925	0.0000
NUMBER_OF_CARS_IN_A_ HOUS	0.465149	0.147945	3.144072	0.0017
TRIP_COST__IN_₹__	−0.049264	0.004162	−11.83742	0.0000
TRIP_TIME__IN_MIN__	−0.012059	0.005847	−2.062531	0.0392

Source: Author's calculation

Limitation of the Model

A passing note on the limitation of the model is supposedly necessary, and the corollary necessity to advance on the same. To begin with, the sample size is required to be enlarged to make the same more representative, and thereby possibly lower the standard deviation value. Also, the exactitude of the collected data can be further enhanced by means of a technology (expressly, Geographic Information System) in order to calculate the distance between a trip origin and trip destination more accurately, as a commuter's response on *trip distance* is typically an approximation. Next, the bivariate model (as done in the present study) can be developed as a multivariate logit model to specifically bring out the probabilities of the alterative travel modes. To end with, Agent Based Modeling (ABM) as well as social network analysis may be further employed to study commuting behavior.

Conclusion

Traffic congestion is expectedly worsening in Kohima. The existing extremely high per capita ownership of car against the context of quantitatively as well as qualitatively inadequate state of the only available PTS spells the salience of supply side intervention as well as demand side intervention; of which, affecting a shift from a personalized mode of transport to a public mode of transport is urgently imperative. For the same, enhancing the existing state of PTS is an immediate requisite in order to mitigate the ongoing traffic congestion as well as the ongoing vehicular air pollution, including the reported spike in trip cost. As suggested in Chapter 2, a scheme of nudging should accompany the said intervention in order to more effectively affect such a shift. Again, in order to bring about an emission easing PTS, the technology powering PTS should be increasingly made green, by means of a mix of policies (such as regulation, subsidies and taxes). As suggested in the preceding chapter 5, given the practicality problem of non-motorized modes owing to the hilly terrain of Kohima, such a provision of PTS is of prime salience to the core elements of sustainable development – economic growth, environmental protection and social inclusion. The feasible policy suggestions from the

112 *Praxis*

survey as well as from the model should be caused to materialize in order to bring about consumer-relevant and effective improvements in urban mobility. Success on the same will contribute towards making Kohima a green engine of regional and international growth.

Notes

1 Standard deviation is a measure of variability of data in a dataset, with a higher value suggesting higher variability, and vice versa.
2 The reported un-served areas by bus include Merhulietsa Colony, Forest Colony, Lerie Colony, AG Colony, Seikhazou Colony, Agri. Colony, Don Bosco/Kohima College Area, New Secretariat, BSF Camp, Aradura, New Reserve, Electrical Colony, Upper/lower Chandmari, Naga Hospital, Para Medical, Kohima Bible College, Jail Colony, Indira Gandhi Stadium, Little Flower School, Billy Graham Road, Old Minister Hill, New Minister Hill, Poterlane Colony, Mission Compound/Bayavu, Naga Bazaar, Chotu Basti, Upper PWD Colony, Lower PWD Colony, Officer Hill Colony and Midlane Colony.
3 100% of the respondents opined that parking is a problem in the city.
4 A construction of a flyover may not be technically as well as financially feasible, however, given the steep slope and geologically unstable terrain.
5 A taxi is hired by an individual and therefore equivalent to a personal car in terms of per capita road space consumption.
6 In the said taxi-sharing, a two-wheeler taxi is excluded given the negligible number of such an observation.

References

Government of India, *Census of India*. Government of India, 2011. http://censusindia. gov.in/

Government of India, *Road transport year book 2013–14, 2014–15 and 2015–16*. Ministry of Road Transport and Highways, New Delhi, 2018.

Qin, Ping, Zheng, Xinye and Wang, Lanlan, *Travel mode choice and impact of fuel tax in Beijing*. Environment and Development Economics, 19, 92–110, 2013.

Part IV

Conclusion

7 Appropriate Urban Policy Making

Introduction

The *State of the World's Cities 2008/2009: Harmonious Cities* of United Nations (2008) elegantly brings out the salience of cities as well as the critical function of planning in making and keeping 'their ascent into greatness':

> Cities contain both order and chaos. In them reside beauty and ugliness, virtue and vice. They can bring out the best or the worst in humankind. They are the physical manifestation of history and culture and incubators of innovation, industry, technology, entrepreneurship and creativity. Cities are the materialization of humanity's noblest ideas, ambitions and aspirations but when not planned or governed properly, can be a repository of society's ills. Cities drive national economies by creating wealth, enhancing social development and providing employment but they can also be the breeding grounds for poverty, exclusion and environmental degradation.

By drawing policy lessons from theory as well as empirics, the ongoing urbanization globally and locally in Kohima can be made as a green resource for sustainable development by means of an apposite urban policy making, and thereby ensure the ascent of Kohima and other cities into greatness.

Urbanization as a Green Resource

At present, on the one hand, urban agglomerations are centres of the wealth of nations owing to the multifarious agglomeration economies that such agglomeration centres occasion. It was so in the past and will be so in the future. What is the case globally is also the case nationally, regionally as well as locally. History, geography and economy of Kohima, a highland city at a frontier, uniquely position it to rapidly emerge as a centre of the wealth of the Indian state of Nagaland as well as of India's NER. On the other hand, urban agglomerations (especially in developing economies) at present are not without challenges owing to the many agglomeration diseconomies. That it is so is seen in the many urban challenges confronting Kohima.

DOI: 10.4324/9781032711799-11

Maximizing the positive externalities as well as minimizing the negative externalities (especially on environment) will enable an optimization of the ongoing urbanization as a green resource for sustainable development. That such an optimization is pragmatically realizable is attested by theoretical expectations as well as empirical substantiations.

In addressing the urban challenges, development and management of urban mobility is indispensably fundamental. An urban mobility system simultaneously addresses the critical binary aspects of any city's development and management: agglomeration economies enhancement on the one hand, and congestion diseconomies mitigation on the other hand. In essence, urban transport development strategy can and ought to address the concerns of growth as well as environment of any city (and thereby of a wider economy).

An optimization attempt of a nature alluded to earlier is therefore made in the context of Kohima so that while economic gains from urban mobility are maximized, environmental losses from urban mobility are minimized. For the same, after analysing the state of economy of Kohima including the condition of urban mobility, policy lessons for urban mobility development and regulatory strategy are drawn from theory as well as empirics.

Kohima: Challenges and Opportunities

A socio-economic profiling as well as a SWOT analysis of Kohima divulges that for myriad potentials, the economic salience of Kohima as an agglomeration centre for the state and the region is immense. Owing to many urban challenges, however, the performance of an otherwise potential regional centre of economic growth is sub-optimal. Of which, an immediate concern is an almost immobile mobility, characterized by supply side inadequacies against the backdrop of a burgeoning demand for urban mobility. The same is also causing an adverse environmental effect (expressly, exacerbating ambient air pollution), and consequently an injurious health effect.

In order to achieve a sustainable growth in Kohima, an urban policy should leverage the strengths and opportunities of the city on the one hand, and mitigate the weaknesses and threats of the city on the other hand. In drawing up such an effective urban policy that is integrated in nature, an understanding of Urban Economics, Transport Economics, Growth Economics and Environment Economics – and an application of the lessons derived thereof against the backdrop of the contextual specificities – is essential.

Lessons From Theory

A survey of the dynamics between and among urban agglomeration, transportation, economic growth and environment reveals a bidirectional nature of interrelationship among the same. In perspective, augmentation in transportation system contributes to economic growth by means of myriad positive externalities that can emanate from the same. It not only engenders cost saving in logistics, trade, transaction and time, but also creates wider economy benefits by means of direct, indirect as well as induced effects on growth. At the same time, however, the converse is also demonstrable. An economic growth engenders the necessary resources to augment a transportation system. Analogously, while a transportation system plays a significant function in the genesis and growth of a city, the later – by contributing to economic growth – provides the required capital to invest in the former, augmenting agglomeration economies and mitigating congestion diseconomies.

The interrelated nature of the relationship among the variables should be appreciated in urban policy making. An acknowledgement of such a relationship entails a comprehensively integrated urban policy making. A land-use planning (including building regulation) should not be carried out in isolation with a transport planning, and vice versa. The negative environmental impacts of commuting – which do not constitute as *cost* from an individual viewpoint are nonetheless *cost* of salience from societal standpoint – need to be incorporated in an individual commuting decision by means of policy intervention. Such a policy to bring about environmental enhancement should be made with developmental considerations and accompanied with nudging scheme (including environmental information dissemination). In essence, a comprehensive urban planning integrating growth concerns as well as environmental concerns is imperative to engender a sustainable city.

In the context of an almost immobile Kohima's urban mobility (as highlighted earlier), anticipatory urban planning and congestion easing supply side interventions thereof (such as segregation of regional traffic from urban traffic by means of bypass) should precede congestion management demand side intervention for welfare, practicality and other suchlike rationales. Of such supply side intervention, an adequate supply of PTS in quantity (especially to cater to the un-served areas) as well as in quality (especially to induce a shift away from congestion accentuating private cars and taxis to congestion easing PTS) is in the main immediately imperative for a sustainable development of the highland city.

On the whole, in conjunction with an environmental consideration, congestion mitigation should be effected considering developmental and welfare dimensions. Such a nature of comprehensive policy exercise is in accordance with an imperative of an apposite growth path, or a growing economy in a salubrious environment.

Lessons From Empirics

What emerges strongly from a survey of literature is that feasible inputs from commuters should be incorporated in SSM as well as DSM in order to bring about consumer-relevant (and therefore more effective) enhancement in urban mobility. Against the backdrop of a severe state of congestion in Kohima, an econometric travel mode choice model is conceived based on primary data. A policy implication that emerges from the results of the model is that, while a congestion easing PTS accessible within a walkable distance that takes a reduced trip time as well as a reduced trip cost should be made available, a congestion accentuating mode of car should be reduced by incorporating suggestions made on the same by the commuters (such as an implementation of an odd and even rationing of car as well as a rationing of car ownership per household). Given the practicality problem of non-motorized modes owing to the hilly terrain of Kohima, such a provision of PTS is of prime salience to the core elements of sustainable development – economic growth, environmental protection and social inclusion. A green mass urban mobility system should be therefore introduced (say, by means of a green technological intervention).

Such a sustainable urban mobility will contribute towards making Kohima an economically productive, environmentally sustainable and socially inclusive urban agglomeration. The ongoing urbanization in the city can then be leveraged as a green resource for sustainable development of the state as well as of the region. The theoretical expectations from the same as well as the empirical evidence on the same have been already discussed in the preceding Part II. Appropriate designing (and prompt implementation) of policy is immediately imperative. In case of a policy failure to suitably intervene, the current concerns confronting the city (highlighted in the previous Part III) will go from bad to worse, and take the potential green engine of growth to a grinding halt.

Directions for Future Research

A research that combines Growth Economics, Urban Economics, Transport Economics and Environmental Economics to draw policy lessons is scant. Given the absence of such an ample theoretical and empirical research on the subject, the book suggests in the main that urban mobility development and management interventions need to simultaneously address the concerns of economic growth and environment. Future research may further explore the multiple aspects of an urban development and regulatory strategy by means of an interdisciplinary approach in the overall context of addressing the concerns of economic growth and environmental management. SWOT analysis can serve as an initial study for further specific and dynamic empirical analysis of the concerns identified in the said study. Underscoring the inadequacy of SSM as well as DSM to bring about consumer-relevant developments in urban mobility, and the salience of incorporating feasible inputs from commuters thereof, an inclusion of ethnographic vignette can be made to comprehensively capture commuters' viewpoints in policy research.

Reference

United Nations, *State of the world's cities 2008/2009: harmonious cities*. Earthscan, Oxford, 2008.

Index

120   *Index*